BREAD MACHINE COOKBOOK

Quick And Easy Recipes For Homemade Bread To Amaze Your Family. Baking Creations, Gluten-Free, Low-Carb Choices & More

GEORGE HARRINGTON

CONTENTS

BASIC BREADS

CAKES AND QUICK BREADS

SAVORY BREADS

FRUIT, VEGETABLE, HERBED & SPICED BREADS

GLUTEN-FREE BREADS

INTERNATIONAL BREADS

Copyright

Introduction

Who Is This Book For?

If you have just purchased, or already own, a bread maker, then you need this book! Here's why:

Get the Most Out of Your Bread Maker!

Illustrated instructions, a quick-start guide and beyond-the-manual tips and tricks will teach you how to get the most out of your bread maker, so that it becomes your family's favorite kitchen appliance.

Learn Fast With Our "10 Minute Quick-Start"

Our illustrated "10 Minute Quick-Start" chapter will walk you through your first bread loaf in under 10 minutes, so you can quickly enjoy delicious, hot, homemade bread, instead of spending all of your time reading instruction manuals.

Clear, Illustrated Instructions

Our instructions will make using a bread maker so simple that you can start baking bread in minutes, while avoiding beginner mistakes such as missed steps, wrong ingredients, soggy crust, etc.

Go Beyond the Instruction Manual

Our pro tips will have you making bread like the pros in no time. Learn the science behind the perfect loaf so that you can confidently make the best, most nutritious bread you've ever had.

Unbiased Recommendations, Workarounds and Pro Tips

These will help you confidently make breads that are perfectly tailored to your family, while avoiding common mistakes.

All the Recipes You'll Ever Need!

101 of the best recipes on the planet will allow you to make the classic breads you are already familiar with, as well as fun and exciting breads that will give your family the variety they love.

ABOUT BREAD MAKERS

What is a Bread Maker?

Human beings have been making bread manually for thousands of years, but now you can make perfect loaves with ease using a bread maker. Modern bread makers take almost all of the guesswork out of making perfect bread in your own home: they automatically regulate mixing, kneading, time and temperature — every step of the bread making process — so all you have to do is decide which ingredients you want to use.

What Does a Bread Maker Do?

The brilliance of a bread maker is that it does all of the work for you: from reminding you to add ingredients, to mixing and kneading. Bread makers allow you to add your favorite ingredients and choose exactly how you want your bread to come out. Their simple settings even allow you to customize your bread to your taste. Best of all, they perform the most time-consuming and labor-intensive aspect of bread making: kneading. With a bread maker you don't have to spend time sweating over your dough because it does all of the kneading for you. And once it has finished preparing the perfect dough, it starts cooking. All you have to do is sit back and enjoy the aroma of freshly baking bread.

What Does a Bread Maker NOT Do?

Because of the size of your bread maker, you will not be able to make certain loaf shapes like baguettes and round country loaves. Additionally, bread makers are designed to allow bread dough to rise and bake. As a result, your bread maker is not ideal for making flat-bread or other types of non-leavened bread. However, you can still use your bread maker to blend and knead your dough for these types of bread and then bake them in a conventional oven.

Who Uses Bread Makers?

Because bread makers typically make large, 1 1/2- and 2-pound loaves, they are perfect for families who use a lot of bread every week. Another reason families love bread makers is that you can have the perfect bread for any situation. Adults often prefer the richness of darker crust, while children like light crusts. With your bread maker you can have either type of crust with the touch of a button. Bread makers make it easy with simple-to-use controls that allow you to choose what type of bread you would prefer (basic, French, sweet, etc.), as well as the level of crust you would like.

The History of Bread Making

Bread is the most common food in the world because it contains vital nutrition and it can be made with a wide variety of different ingredients. Basically, wherever you live you can find ingredients to make bread. Because of this, humans have been making bread from various ingredients for around 30,000 years. Before we figured out how to make leavened bread, flatbreads were common in many parts of the world. A little over 2,000 years ago, bakers in the Middle East figured out that by adding yeast, a natural leavener, they could make fluffy loaves that allowed their ingredients to go further. For many years (possibly millennia), bread was sold in whole, unsliced loaves. Then in 1917, a jeweler named Otto Rohwedder invented a machine that automatically sliced a whole loaf of bread in seconds. It was the greatest thing since... well, sliced bread. Within two years of his invention, almost all bread sold in American stores was pre-sliced.

The modern bread machine came along in 1986, when the company which would become Panasonic introduced the first machine that allowed people to make bread at home without doing nearly as much work. Over time, bread makers became more compact and more functional. Today's bread-making machines are capable of making a much wider array of breads and do even more of the work. Modern bread machines are perfect for families looking to save some money and to make breads the whole family will love. You can customize the ingredients you use to ensure that your bread is nutritious as well as delicious. And since a lot of commercial breads are packed with sugar and hard-to-pronounce chemicals, you can use your bread maker to bake loaves that are healthier, just like the bread made thousands of years ago.

Health Benefits

Many people are concerned about the role that carbohydrates play in weight gain and diabetes, and rightly so. Unfortunately, that means sometimes avoiding things like bread. But by making your own bread, that doesn't have to be the case. While commercial bread may be packed with extra sugar, low-grade flour or even chemicals, the bread you make at home in your bread maker can be so much healthier while still being delicious. From limiting added sugar, to using protein-boosting sourdough starter, to adding healthy nuts and whole grains, you can make bread that is packed with nutrition and flavor. And best of all, you can make bread packed with real, wholesome ingredients, instead of sugars and chemicals. Many bread makers even have a specific gluten-free function, which allows you to make the best quality gluten-free loaves.

Cautions

Because your bread maker has a powerful motor to ensure perfectly blended dough, the machine should always be placed on a firm, flat surface. To prevent the unit from moving during mixing, we also recommend that you place a kitchen towel under the unit to help keep it firmly in place. The machine's powerful motor, combined with an automatic kneading function, means children should ALWAYS be supervised when helping out. The turning kneading blade produces a perfectly even dough, but you need to make sure children do not put their hands in the machine while the kneading function is activated.

HOW TO USE A BREAD MAKER

Equipment You Will Need

Because your bread maker is so wonderfully self-contained, you won't need a lot of extra equipment to start making amazing bread. Most likely, your bread maker will include things like cooking pans, but you will want to make sure you also have a good-quality cooling rack for your freshly baked bread - placing hot loaves on a flat surface can trap steam on the underside of the bread, leading to a soggy bottom. And because the one thing your bread maker does not do is slice your bread, you will want to make sure to have a nice, sharp bread knife. Regular knives are usually not serrated and they will have a hard time cleanly cutting the loaf. A bread knife has a wide serrated pattern that allows you to easily saw through the loaf and produce perfectly even slices, no matter what kind of bread you are slicing.

Setting Up and Using Your Bread Maker

Remove your bread maker from its box and place on a flat surface, ideally a firm countertop with enough overhead clearance to easily open the top all the way. At this point, leave the bread maker unplugged. Open the top of the bread maker and remove the baking pan by holding the handle and pulling straight up. Make sure to gently wash the baking pan with warm water and soap to remove any chemical residue before using the first time. Attach the kneading blade to the baking pan and make sure it is firmly in place. The kneading blade isn't sharp, but it will become hot during the baking process, so be careful when handling it right after baking.

LEARNING THE CONTROLS

While bread makers vary slightly depending on the brand, most will have the following functions which will allow you to make many different types of bread:

Cycle button: This button allows you to choose what kind of bread you want to make. **Choose from**: Basic, French, Gluten Free, Quick, Sweet, Dough, Jam, and Cake. Continue pressing the Select button to scroll through the options.

Crust Color button: Your bread maker allows you to choose from three different crust color options: Light, Medium, and Dark. Continue to press this button to scroll through the darkness options.

Loaf Size: Using this button to choose between making a 1.5-pound loaf or a 2-pound loaf.

Display: The LCD display allows you to see your current baking settings. You can see the type of bread you are making and the color setting, as well as the time remaining in the baking cycle.

Delay Time: If you don't want to make your bread immediately, you can adjust the amount of time until the bread maker begins kneading/baking.

Start/Stop: If you want to make bread right away, pressing this will begin the baking process.

The Cooking Process

Because bread making is a complicated scientific process, it's important to understand what your bread maker is doing during the baking process. This will allow you to make loaves that turn out perfectly every time you bake!

•**Mixing Yeast** : As soon as you add yeast to your other ingredients, the process begins. Yeast is actually a living organism that occurs naturally all over the world (it's even in the air!).¬ When the ingredients are mixed, the yeast begins releasing carbon dioxide, which is what allows bread to rise and form bubbles.

•**Kneading**: Your bread maker doesn't just bake bread, it also does the hard work of kneading the dough as well. This part of the process used to take time and a lot of effort, but luckily, your bread maker makes this step as easy as pressing the Start button. Once the kneading begins, the bread maker will begin combining all of the ingredients in an even manner. In order to get evenly baked bread, the ingredients need to be evenly incorporated. This step is also important in forming gluten, which is the protein that makes bread chewy and fluffy.

Note:If you are using gluten-free ingredients, then this step will not form gluten

•**Rising:** Once the kneading is finished, your bread maker will allow the dough to rise for the appropriate amount of time. During this time, the yeast will have an opportunity to create more bubbles, which will then allow the bread to rise to its proper height when baked. Because it is hard to know just how long to allow your dough to rise, the bread maker is programmed to know exactly how much rising will produce a perfect loaf.

•**Baking**: After the dough has had enough time to rise, the baking process automatically begins, and the bread maker will bake the bread for the optimal amount of time, depending on what kind of bread you are making, and your individual preferences.

Troubleshooting

PROBLEM	SOLUTION
My bread didn't rise.	There may be several reasons why your bread didn't rise, but the most common reason is that you have not added enough yeast. Try increasing the yeast by 20%.
I added more yeast and my bread still didn't rise.	Yeast is a living organism and because of this it has a finite lifespan. Check to see how old your yeast is. If it's getting close to the expiration date it may be too old to work properly.
The top of my bread isn't thoroughly cooked.	If the top of your bread is raw, it is because it touched the top of your bread maker. This is usually caused by adding too much yeast to the dough. As a result, the bread rises too much. Next time, reduce the amount of yeast by 20%.
My dough feels too wet and sticky (prior to baking).	You need to add some extra flour to the dough. As the bread maker kneads the bread, add in flour one teaspoon at a time until the dough is no longer sticky.
When I cut into my bread it has giant bubbles in it.	These bubbles are caused by your yeast creating too much air as the bread cooks. Next time, reduce your yeast by 20%.
When I cut into my bread, it's really dense.	If your bread is too dense, that means the dough was too dry before baking. Next time, check the dough before baking. If it is too dry, try adding water one teaspoon at a time until it loosens up.
I just made whole wheat bread and it tastes like it's gone bad.	Unlike white flour, whole wheat flour contains parts of the wheat that can become rancid when stored at room temperature. To avoid this problem, store whole wheat flours in the refrigerator or freezer.

10 MINUTE QUICK-START

The goal of 10 Minute Quick-Start is to walk you through making your first loaf so you "learn by doing" in under 10 minutes. Once you've had a chance to get familiar with how your bread maker works, you can begin experimenting with different types of loaves.

Let's get started!

Overview

Getting perfect results with your first loaf of bread can be difficult.

Luckily, baking bread with a bread maker takes most of the guesswork out of it. Let's start by making a simple white bread. This loaf uses the simplest ingredients and the most basic settings on your Bread Maker, yet results in a mouthwateringly delicious, fresh-baked bread loaf that will make your family jump for joy.

Collect These Ingredients:

- 1-1/8 cup water
- 2 tablespoons oil (vegetable or olive)
- 2 tablespoons sugar
- 1 teaspoon salt
- 3 cups bread flour
- 4 1/2 teaspoons quick rise yeast

Collect These Tools:

- Your bread maker
- Measuring cups
- Tablespoon
- Teaspoon
- Thermometer
- Cooling rack (or a place to place the finished loaf to cool)

Follow These Instructions:

1. Measure 1 cup plus 2 tablespoons of water heated to between 115°F and 125°F. Pour the water into the baking pan.
2. Add oil to the water.
3. Add sugar, salt, and bread flour (bread flour is different from all-purpose flour), then add quick rise yeast.
4. Place the baking pan into the bread maker and press the Cycle button until you reach "Basic."
5. Press the Start/Stop button and your bread maker will begin kneading and baking bread.
6. When the baking is finished, remove the baking pan from the machine and place upside down on a cooling rack. Tap

the pan several times until the bread slides out. The non-stick coating on the baking pan will make this easy.

7. Allow the bread to cool before slicing and enjoying your first loaf!

CONGRATULATIONS!

You've just made your first loaf and learned the basics of how to use your bread maker. Time to celebrate! Give yourself a pat on the back, and enjoy some extra butter (or whatever your love most) with fresh hot bread!

Know Your Types of Bread

White bread
All purpose flour, mild flavor, soft texture.

Focaccia
Chewy and salty, great for topping.

Wheat bread
Mixture of whole wheat flour and bread flour, nutty flavor, high in nutrition.

Sourdough
Dense and chewy. Made with bread flour and sourdough starter.

Multigrain bread
Bread flour and grains, dense texture, earthy flavor.

Rye
Dense and tangy, bread flour and rye flour, caraway seeds for extra flavor.

French bread
Crispy crust, bread flour, sourdough starter for tangy flavor.

Pumpernickel
Dark and dense, higher percentage of rye flour.

Ciabatta
Chewy texture from bread flour and olive oil, mild flavor.

PRO TIPS

Why Water Temperature Matters

More than any other type of cooking, baking is a science and every detail matters. Your bread maker takes care of a lot of the science of baking bread, but there are still a few important factors under your control that will determine how successfully your bread turns out. The ingredient which determines how well your bread rises, and thus how well it turns out, is yeast. Because yeast is a living organism, it only does its job correctly under certain specific conditions. This is why water temperature is so important. If the water is too cold the yeast will be sluggish, and it won't produce enough carbon dioxide. This will lead to loaves that don't rise enough, and have a dense, doughy consistency. If your water is too warm, it will kill the yeast, and this often leads to even less rising. In order to get the best results, you will want to use a kitchen thermometer and make sure your water is between 115°F and 125°F. Water heated to within this range provides the perfect environment for the yeast to activate and do its job. Also, be sure to keep track of how old your yeast is. Because it is a living organism, it will eventually die and won't be able to produce carbon dioxide. All yeast packages have an expiration date. If your yeast has passed, or is even close to, that date, throw it away and buy some fresh yeast.

SELECTING THE RIGHT KIND OF YEAST

There are many different types of yeast out there and choosing the correct one can be a challenge. Yeast is a naturally occurring organism, and it is the main ingredient used by bread makers to make leavened breads. Prior to the discovery of yeast, all bread was flatbread. The best type of yeast to use for most applications with your bread maker is quick-rise yeast. This differs from traditional active dry yeast because it activates even faster and produces carbon dioxide at a faster rate. In general, most of the yeast you will use to make bread with your bread maker will be dry yeast, however, there is one type of bread which gets its signature flavor from a wet type of yeast: sourdough. Sourdough is the oldest form of leavened bread and it is made using a wet "starter," rather than powdered yeast. You can make your own starter at home or purchase dry starter and hydrate it and feed it to keep it active.

BREAD FLOUR VS. ALL-PURPOSE FLOUR

Just like there are different types of yeast, there are different types of flour that will produce different types of bread. In general, it is recommended to use bread flour when baking in your bread maker, but depending on what type of loaf you want to make, this is not always the case. Bread flour is higher in protein than all-purpose flour, and as a result, bread made with bread flour has a higher gluten content. This will result in loaves that are chewier and denser than bread made with all-purpose flour. So, if you are trying to make a chewy French loaf, bread flour is certainly the way to go. However, a classic white bread or brioche may be lighter and fluffier with all-purpose flour.

WEIGHT VS. VOLUME

In most cooking, using volume as a measure is perfectly fine, however, because baking is more of an exact science, the best way to get perfect results is by using weight to measure your ingredients, rather than volume. Over the years, bakers narrowed their measurements down to exact weights rather than volumes. However, because not everyone has easy access to scales, those weights were converted to volumes because more people had things handy like measuring spoons and cups. If you want to maximize your results, invest in a simple kitchen scale and follow the directions for weight rather than volume. If you do not want to use a kitchen scale, just be sure to use quality measuring utensils. Many cheaper measuring cups or spoons are not accurate, and this may negatively affect your final product.

Master the Moisture in Your Dough

In order to get the very best results when making bread, it is important to make sure your dough has the correct moisture content. This will affect how well the bread rises and how evenly it cooks. Traditionally, bakers have kneaded bread dough by hand and it was easy to keep track of how moist the dough was at any given time. Because your bread maker does all of the kneading for you, you won't have as much contact with the dough, but that doesn't mean that you can't inspect it to make sure it has the proper moisture. During the kneading cycle, check the dough. If it is soggy and not holding together, add some flour until the consistency becomes more firm. You should also add a little flour if the dough feels sticky to the touch or if dough comes off on your fingers when you touch it. Conversely, if the dough feels flaky or floury to the touch, add a little water until it becomes smooth and elastic.

How to tell if the dough is perfect: Poke it with your finger. Ideally, your dough should bounce back quickly when you poke it.

EXPERIMENTING WITH FLOURS

In addition to bread flour and all-purpose flour, you can also experiment with whole wheat flour, which will result in a dense yet nutty flavor that is a great source of nutrition. By experimenting with different ratios of whole wheat to bread flour you can customize the perfect level of whole wheat, from just a slight hint to a very dense and nutritious loaf. You can also buy rye flour for mixing with either all-purpose or bread flour, for a hearty and tangy rye bread. The addition of a tablespoon of caraway seeds will give you a really authentic, deli-style rye bread. Since there is such a wide variety of different flours on the market now, you can experiment with adding many different types of flour. We recommend adding small amounts of nut flour like almond flour for an extra hint of flavor.

Make Pasta with Your Bread Maker

While you won't be baking the pasta in the bread maker, you can take advantage of its powerful motor to take a lot of the effort out of making fresh pasta. Because pasta dough needs extensive kneading to come out smooth and even, you can place all of your pasta dough ingredients (flour, eggs, salt, and a bit of olive oil) into the baking pan and use the dough/pasta function to effortlessly knead your dough to perfection. When it is finished kneading, remove the dough from the machine and wrap in plastic wrap. Place the dough on a countertop and allow to rest for about a half an hour. This will give the ingredients time to fully incorporate before you roll it and cut it.

ADDING INGREDIENTS TO YOUR BREAD

Once your bread maker has combined your bread ingredients, you will have an opportunity to add different ingredients to your bread dough. Chopped nuts and dried fruit make an excellent addition and will impart an interesting flavor and texture to your bread. You can also try adding things like chopped olives and fresh herbs, for earthy and delicious loaves that work wonderfully as a base for a sandwich or as a wholesome snack. Another fun way to add ingredients to your bread is by making sweet breads like cinnamon raisin or cranberry orange. Simply sprinkle in a bit of cinnamon mixed with sugar and a handful or raisins, or add dried cranberries with a teaspoon of fresh orange zest. Once you get started using your bread maker you will find that the possibilities for amazing, healthy, and creative breads are nearly limitless!

BASIC BREADS

The Easiest Bread Maker Bread

Baking fresh bread can be super-easy and fun right in the comfort of your own kitchen. This easy-to-use recipe will have you baking like a pro in less time than traditional bread recipes. Great served warm with butter or as sandwich bread, you'll love this delicious beginner's bread.

SERVINGS: 12 | PREP TIME: 5 MINUTES | COOK TIME: 3 HOURS

INGREDIENTS:

- 1 cup lukewarm water
- 1/3 cup lukewarm milk
- 3 tablespoons butter, unsalted
- 3 3/4 cups unbleached all-purpose flour
- 3 tablespoons sugar
- 1 1/2 teaspoons salt
- 1 1/2 teaspoons active dry yeast

DIRECTIONS:

1. Add liquid ingredients to the bread pan.
2. Measure and add dry ingredients (except yeast) to the bread pan.
3. Make a well in the center of the dry ingredients and add the yeast .
4. Snap the baking pan into the bread maker and close the lid.
5. Choose the Basic setting, preferred crust color and press Start.
6. When the loaf is done, remove the pan from the machine. After about 5 minutes, gently shake the pan to loosen the loaf and turn it out onto a rack to cool.
7. Store bread, well-wrapped, on the counter up to 4 days, or freeze for up to 3 months.

NUTRITIONAL INFO: CALORIES: 183, SODIUM: 316 MG, DIETARY Fiber: 1.2 g, Fat: 3.3 g, Carbs: 33.3 g, Protein: 4.5 g.

100% Whole Wheat Bread

Whole wheat bread is 100% delicious and nutritious. This soft-baked bread is also great for those who are on a heart healthy diet. Serve it toasted with butter and jam for breakfast or alongside a delicious bowl of soup for a hearty meal.

SERVINGS: 12 | PREP TIME: 10 MINUTES | COOK TIME: 3 HOURS 30 MINUTES

INGREDIENTS:

- 1 cup warm water
- 2 tablespoons butter
- 1 teaspoon salt
- 3 cups 100% whole wheat flour
- 2 tablespoons dry milk
- 1 tablespoon sugar
- 2 teaspoons active dry yeast

DIRECTIONS:

1. Add the liquid ingredients to the bread maker.
2. Add the dry ingredients, except the yeast.
3. Make a well in the center of the bread flour and add the yeast.
4. Insert the pan into your bread maker and secure the lid.
5. Select Wheat Bread setting, choose your preferred crust color and press Start.
6. Remove the bread from the oven and turn it out of the pan onto a wire rack and allow it to cool completely before slicing.

NUTRITIONAL INFO: CALORIES: 126, SODIUM: 211 MG, DIETARY Fiber: 3.8 g, Fat: 2.6 g, Carbs: 23.2 g, Protein: 4.5 g.

Brioche

One of the most quintessentially French breakfast breads is brioche. It is light, airy, and delicious served with jam and butter. It is also easy to make with a little help from your bread maker!

SERVINGS: 12 | PREP TIME: 20 MINUTES | COOK TIME: 2 HOURS

INGREDIENTS:

- 1/4 cup milk
- 2 eggs
- 4 tablespoons butter
- 1 1/2 tablespoons vanilla sugar
- 1/4 teaspoon salt
- 2 cups flour
- 1 1/2 teaspoon yeast
- 1 egg white, for finishing

DIRECTIONS:

1. Place wet ingredients (except egg white for finishing) into your bread machine.
2. Add dry ingredients, except for yeast.
3. Make a well inside the flour and then add the yeast into the well.
4. Set to Dough cycle and press Start.
5. Remove dough, place dough on floured surface and divide into 12 equal size rolls.
6. Pinch walnut-sized ball of dough off each roll, making a smaller ball; make indent on top of roll and wet with milk; attach small ball to top making the traditional brioche shape.
7. Let rise for 30 minutes until almost double in size.
8. Preheat oven to 375°F.
9. Beat egg white, brush tops of brioche rolls, and bake at 375°F for 10 to 12 minutes, or until golden on top. Cool on rach before serving.

NUTRITIONAL INFO: CALORIES: 180, SODIUM: 120 MG, DIETARY Fiber: 0.7 g, Fat: 0.9 g, Carbs: 16.9 g, Protein: 2.6 g.

Crusty Sourdough Bread

Nothing hits the spot like a loaf of crusty sourdough bread. Perfect on a cold winter day with fresh homemade soup - this loaf is easy to make and delicious too!

SERVINGS 12 | PREP TIME: 20 MINUTES | COOK TIME: 3 HOURS 45 MINUTES

INGREDIENTS:
Sourdough Starter:

- 1 1/2 teaspoons quick active dry yeast
- 4 cups warm water
- 3 cups all-purpose flour
- 4 teaspoons sugar

Bread:

- 1/2 cup water

- 3 cups bread flour
- 2 tablespoons sugar
- 1 1/2 teaspoons salt
- 1 teaspoon quick active dry yeast

DIRECTIONS:

1. Prepare the sourdough starter at least one week before baking the bread by dissolving 1 1/2 teaspoons yeast in warm water in a glass bowl.
2. Stir in 3 cups flour and the 4 teaspoons sugar. Beat with electric mixer on medium speed for 1 minute or until smooth.
3. Cover loosely and let stand at room temperature for one week or until mixture is bubbly and has a sour aroma; when ready, cover tight and refrigerate until ready to use.
4. When you are ready to bake the bread, measure out 1 cup of the sourdough starter and all of the remaining bread ingredients carefully, placing in bread machine pan the wet ingredients first, then dry ingredients.
5. Select Basic and Medium Crust, then press Start.
6. Remove baked bread from pan and cool on a wire rack.

NUTRITIONAL INFO: CALORIES: 216, SODIUM: 295 MG, DIETARY Fiber: 1.6 g, Fat: 0.6 g, Carbs: 45.8 g, Protein: 6.6 g.

Basic White Bread

Soft white bakery style bread is absolutely delicious and quick to whip up in a bread maker. You'll love baking fresh loaves to serve as toast with breakfast or as the perfect complement to your favorite sandwich ingredients and condiments.

SERVINGS: 16 | PREP TIME: 10 MINUTES | COOK TIME: 3 HOURS

INGREDIENTS:

- 1 cup warm water
- 2 tablespoons agave nectar
- 1/4 cup applesauce
- 3 cups bread flour
- 1 teaspoon salt
- 2 1/4 teaspoons rapid rise yeast

DIRECTIONS:

1. Add liquid ingredients to the bread pan.
2. Measure and add dry ingredients (except yeast) to the bread pan.
3. Make a well in the center of the dry ingredients and add the yeast.
4. Snap the baking pan into the bread maker and close the lid.
5. Choose the Basic setting, preferred crust color and press Start.
6. Remove and allow to cool on a wire rack when baked, before serving.

NUTRITIONAL INFO: CALORIES: 92, SODIUM: 148 MG, DIETARY Fiber: 0.9 g, Fat: 0.3 g, Carbs: 19.5 g, Protein: 2.6 g.

Basic Wheat Bread

Wheat bread is a delicious alternative to white and great for anyone on a diabetic or low-cholesterol diet. Baking this healthier bread is just as easy as making a loaf of white bread, and it can still be enjoyed with soups, breakfast, and in a sandwich.

SERVINGS: 12 | PREP TIME: 10 MINUTES | COOK TIME: 2 HOURS

INGREDIENTS:

- 1 1/2 cups warm water
- 1/2 cup honey
- 1 tablespoon olive oil
- 1 teaspoon sea salt
- 3 cups wheat flour
- 1 cup bread flour, unbleached
- 2 teaspoons active dry yeast

DIRECTIONS:

1. Mix dry ingredients together in a bowl, except for yeast.
2. Add wet ingredients to bread pan first; top with dry ingredients.
3. Make a well in the center of the dry ingredients and add the yeast.
4. Choose the Wheat Bread setting, preferred crust color and press Start.
5. Remove and allow to cool on a wire rack when baked, before serving.

NUTRITIONAL INFO: CALORIES: 75, SODIUM: 60 MG, DIETARY FIBER: 0.5 g, Fat: 0.6 g, Carbs: 15.8 g, Protein: 1.8 g.

Honey Wheat Bread

This scrumptious recipe is just the way to go when you love wheat bread with a touch of honey. Serve it warm with butter and a drizzle of honey or jam for a sweet breakfast or afternoon treat.

SERVINGS: 12 | PREP TIME: 10 MINUTES | COOK TIME: 3 HOURS 30 MINUTES

INGREDIENTS:

- 4 1/2 cups 100% whole wheat flour
- 1 1/2 cups warm water
- 1/3 cup olive oil
- 1/3 cup honey
- 2 teaspoons salt
- 1 tablespoon active dry yeast

DIRECTIONS:

1. Add water to the bread maker.
2. Measure and add the oil first, then the honey in the same measuring cup: this will make the honey slip out of the measuring cup more easily.
3. Add salt, then flour.
4. Make a small well in the flour and add the yeast.
5. Set to Wheat Bread, choose crust color, and press Start.
6. Remove and allow to cool on a wire rack when baked, before serving.

NUTRITIONAL INFO: CALORIES: 232, SODIUM: 392 MG, DIETARY Fiber: 5.7 g, Fat: 6.5 g, Carbs: 40.8 g, Protein: 6.6 g.

Rye Bread

Rye bread is absolutely delicious when used as the base of a scrumptious Reuben sandwich. You can also toast this robust bread and use it as a bruschetta base for a delicious snack or hors d'oeuvre at your next party.

SERVINGS: 12 | PREP TIME: 5 MINUTES | COOK TIME: 3 HOURS

INGREDIENTS:

- 1 cup water
- 1 1/2 teaspoons salt
- 2 tablespoons sugar
- 1 tablespoon butter
- 2 teaspoons caraway seed
- 2 cups bread flour
- 1 cup rye flour
- 1 1/2 teaspoons quick active yeast

DIRECTIONS:

1. Place all of the ingredients except yeast in the bread maker pan in the order listed.
2. Make a well in the center of the dry ingredients and add the yeast.
3. Choose the Basic cycle for 1 1/25-pound loaf and medium crust color. Press Start.
4. Remove bread when done and allow to cool for 10 minutes before slicing with a bread knife.

NUTRITIONAL INFO: CALORIES: 129, SODIUM: 299 MG, DIETARY Fiber: 3.2 g, Fat: 1.5 g, Carbs: 25.6 g, Protein: 4 g.

Potato Bread

When you want a sweet, dense bread this recipe is absolutely delicious and easy to make. Flavorful and moist, you'll transform any meal with a thick slice of this yummy potato bread.

SERVINGS: 12 | PREP TIME: 10 MINUTES | COOK TIME: 3 HOURS

INGREDIENTS:

- 3/4 cup water
- 2/3 cup instant mashed potatoes
- 1 egg
- 2 tablespoons butter, unsalted
- 2 tablespoons white sugar
- 1/4 cup dry milk powder
- 1 teaspoon salt
- 3 cups bread flour
- 1 1/2 teaspoons active dry yeast

DIRECTIONS:

1. Add the ingredients to bread maker in the order listed above. Reserve yeast for next step.
2. Make a well in the center of the dry ingredients and add the yeast.
3. Press Basic bread cycle, choose light to medium crust color, and press Start.
4. Remove from bread pan and allow to cool on a wire rack before serving.

NUTRITIONAL INFO: CALORIES: 165, SODIUM: 231 MG, DIETARY Fiber: 1.1 g, Fat: 2.6 g, Carbs: 29.7 g, Protein: 5.2 g.

Pumpernickel Bread

A heavy, sweet loaf, pumpernickel bread is a delicious alternative to regular bread as it is cholesterol free and low in fat. Great for those counting calories too, as it only contains 65 calories per slice. Fresh baked, this delicious bread will soon become a healthy eating favorite.

SERVINGS: 12 | PREP TIME: 5 MINUTES | COOK TIME: 3 HOURS 30 MINUTES

INGREDIENTS:

- 1 1/4 cups lukewarm water
- 1/4 cup molasses
- 2 tablespoons unsweetened cocoa powder
- 1 teaspoon sea salt
- 1 cup whole wheat flour
- 1 cup rye flour
- 2 cups unbleached all-purpose flour
- 2 1/2 tablespoons vegetable oil

- 1 1/2 tablespoons packed brown sugar
- 1 tablespoon caraway seeds
- 2 1/2 teaspoons instant yeast

DIRECTIONS:

1. Note: all ingredients should be at room temperature before baking.
2. Add all of the ingredients in the order listed above, reserving yeast.
3. Make a well in the center of the dry ingredients and add the yeast .
4. Set the bread maker on Whole Wheat cycle, select crust color, and press Start.
5. Remove and let the loaf cool for 15 minutes before slicing.

NUTRITIONAL INFO: CALORIES: 263, SODIUM: 160 MG, DIETARY Fiber: 4.7 g, Fat: 3.5 g, Carbs: 50.6 g, Protein: 7.1 g.

Multigrain Bread

Multigrain bread is a delicious alternative to wheat bread and offers you a more well-rounded serving of grains. You'll love this seeded bread toasted for breakfast with butter and jam or as the base of all your favorite sandwiches.

SERVINGS: 12 | PREP TIME: 5 MINUTES | COOK TIME: 3 HOURS

INGREDIENTS:

- 2 1/4 cups whole wheat flour
- 3/4 cup ground oatmeal
- 2 tablespoons wheat bran
- 2 tablespoons flaxseed meal
- 2 tablespoons vital wheat gluten
- 1 tablespoon dough enhancer
- 1 teaspoon salt
- 2 2/3 teaspoons active dry yeast

- 2 tablespoons olive oil
- 1 tablespoon agave nectar
- 1 tablespoon brown sugar
- 1 cup warm water (slightly warmer than room temperature)

DIRECTIONS:

1. Set the yeast aside and combine the remaining dry ingredients in a mixing bowl.
2. Add the liquids to the bread maker first, followed by the dry ingredients.
3. Make a small well in the flour and add the yeast.
4. Press Whole Wheat cycle, light crust color, and press Start.
5. Remove loaf when done and lay on a cooling rack until cool to slice.

NUTRITIONAL INFO: CALORIES: 138, SODIUM: 196 MG, DIETARY Fiber: 1.6 g, Fat: 3.2 g, Carbs: 21.9 g, Protein: 5.3 g.

Cracked Wheat Bread

Looking to add healthy fiber to your diet? This delicious cracked wheat bread is just the way to do exactly that without sacrificing your favorite foods, like sandwiches and breakfast toast.

SERVINGS: 10 | PREP TIME: 15 MINUTES | COOK TIME: 1 HOUR 20 MINUTES

INGREDIENTS:

- 1 1/4 cup plus 1 tablespoon water
- 2 tablespoons vegetable oil
- 3 cups bread flour
- 3/4 cup cracked wheat
- 1 1/2 teaspoons salt
- 2 tablespoons sugar
- 2 1/4 teaspoons active dry yeast

DIRECTIONS:

1. Bring water to a boil.
2. Place cracked wheat in small mixing bowl, pour water over it and stir.
3. Cool to 80°F.
4. Place cracked wheat mixture into pan, followed by all ingredients (except yeast) in the order listed.
5. Make a well in the center of the dry ingredients and add the yeast.
6. Select the Basic Bread cycle, medium color crust, and press Start.
7. Check dough consistency after 5 minutes of kneading. The dough should be a soft, tacky ball. If it is dry and stiff, add water one 1/2 tablespoon at a time until sticky. If it's too wet and sticky, add 1 tablespoon of flour at a time.
8. Remove bread when cycle is finished and allow to cool before serving.

NUTRITIONAL INFO: CALORIES: 232, SODIUM: 350 MG, DIETARY Fiber: 3.3 g, Fat: 3.3 g, Carbs: 43.7 g, Protein: 6.3 g.

Pretzel Rolls

Pretzel rolls are a delicious way to serve your favorite sandwiches. Bake them to complement burgers, turkey, ham and swiss, or even tofu burgers.

SERVINGS: 4 | PREP TIME: 25 MINUTES | COOK TIME: 3 HOURS 10 MINUTES

INGREDIENTS:

- 1 cup warm water
- 1 egg white, beaten
- 2 tablespoons oil
- 3 cups all-purpose flour
- 1/2 teaspoon salt
- 1 tablespoon granulated sugar
- 1 package dry yeast
- Coarse sea salt, for topping

- 1/3 cup baking soda (for boiling process, *DO NOT PUT IN THE PRETZEL DOUGH*)
- Flour, for surface

DIRECTIONS:

1. Place the ingredients in bread machine pan in the order listed above, reserving yeast
2. Make a well in the center of the dry ingredients and add the yeast.
3. Select Dough cycle and press Start.
4. Remove the dough out onto a lightly floured surface and divide dough into four parts.
5. Roll the four parts into balls.
6. Place on greased cookie sheet and let rise uncovered for about 20 minutes or until puffy.
7. In a 3-quart saucepan, combine 2 quarts of water and baking soda and bring to a boil.
8. Preheat an oven to 425°F.
9. Lower 2 pretzels into the saucepan and simmer for 10 seconds on each side.
10. Lift from water with a slotted spoon and return to greased cookie sheet; repeat with remaining pretzels.
11. Let dry briefly.
12. Brush with egg white and sprinkle with coarse salt.
13. Bake in preheated oven for 20 minutes or until golden brown.
14. Let cool slightly before serving.

NUTRITIONAL INFO: CALORIES: 422, SODIUM: 547 MG, DIETARY Fiber: 2.9 g, Fat: 7.8 g, Carbs: 75.3 g, Protein: 11.3 g.

Peasant Bread

A basic recipe that is full of flavor, this bread maker peasant bread is sure to please the whole family. Traditionally a before-dinner bread, you can also serve this alongside salads for any dinner party or romantic dinner at home.

SERVINGS: 12 | PREP TIME: 5 MINUTES | COOK TIME: 3 HOURS

INGREDIENTS:

- 2 tablespoons full rounded yeast
- 2 cups white bread flour
- 1 1/2 tablespoons sugar
- 1 tablespoon salt
- 7/8 cup water
- For the topping:
- Olive oil
- Poppy seeds

DIRECTIONS:

1. Add water first, then add the dry ingredients to the bread machine, reserving yeast.
2. Make a well in the center of the dry ingredients and add the yeast.
3. Choose French cycle, light crust color, and push Start.
4. When bread is finished, coat the top of loaf with a little olive oil and lightly sprinkle with poppy seeds.
5. Allow to cool slightly and serve warm with extra olive oil for dipping.

NUTRITIONAL INFO: CALORIES: 87, SODIUM: 583 MG, DIETARY FIBER: 1 g, Fat: 0.3 g, Carbs: 18.2 g, Protein: 2.9 g.

Sweet Dinner Rolls

Nothing makes dinner sweeter than a fresh-baked batch of sweet dinner rolls. Perfect for main dishes like roast beef, duck, or chicken, these dinner rolls are sure to be an absolute hit for any festive meal you serve your family.

SERVINGS: 16 | PREP TIME: 15 MINUTES | COOK TIME: 2 HOUR 20 MINUTES

INGREDIENTS:

- 1/2 cup warm water
- 1/2 cup warm milk
- 1 egg
- 1/3 cup butter, unsalted and softened
- 1/3 cup sugar
- 1 teaspoon salt
- 3 3/4 cups all-purpose flour
- 1 (1/4 ounce) package active dry yeast

- 1/4 cup butter, softened
- Flour, for surface

DIRECTIONS:

1. Place ingredients in the bread pan in the following order: water, milk, egg, butter, sugar, salt, and flour. Reserve yeast.
2. Make a well in the center of the dry ingredients and add the yeast.
3. Select Dough cycle and press Start.
4. When cycle finishes, turn dough out onto a lightly floured surface.
5. Divide dough in half and roll each half into a 12-inch circle, spread 1/4 cup softened butter over entire round. Cut each circle into 8 wedges. Roll wedges starting at the wide end and roll gently but tight.
6. Place point side down on ungreased cookie sheet. Cover with clean kitchen towel and put in a warm place, let rise 1 hour.
7. Preheat oven to 400°F and bake rolls in preheated oven for 10 to 15 minutes, until golden.
8. Serve warm.

NUTRITIONAL INFO: CALORIES: 182, SODIUM: 197 MG, DIETARY Fiber: 0.9 g, Fat: 6.5 g, Carbs: 27.1 g, Protein: 3.9 g.

Southern Cornbread

Southern-style cornbread is deliciously sweet and best served with savory dishes. Eat it buttered on its own, or serve with homemade vegetable soup or pinto beans for one sweet Southern meal!

SERVINGS: 10 | PREP TIME: 5 MINUTES | COOK TIME: 1 HOUR

INGREDIENTS:

- 2 fresh eggs, at room temperature
- 1 cup milk
- 1/4 cup butter, unsalted, at room temperature
- 3/4 cup sugar
- 1 teaspoon salt
- 2 cups unbleached all-purpose flour
- 1 cup cornmeal
- 1 tablespoon baking powder

DIRECTIONS:

1. Add all of the ingredients to your bread maker in the order listed.
2. Select the Quick Bread cycle, light crust color, and press Start.
3. Allow to cool for five minutes on a wire rack and serve warm.

NUTRITIONAL INFO: CALORIES: 258, SODIUM: 295 MG, DIETARY Fiber: 1.6 g, Fat: 6.7 g, Carbs: 45.4 g, Protein: 5.5 g.

Slider Buns

Sliders are delicious little sandwiches you can whip up for little ones at lunch or serve as hors d'oeuvres at any tailgate or party. The stuffing choices for slider sandwiches are endless once you master this delicious basic bun recipe.

SERVINGS: 18 | PREP TIME: 15 MINUTES | COOK TIME: 3 HOURS

INGREDIENTS:

- 1 1/4 cups milk
- 1 egg
- 2 tablespoons butter
- 3/4 teaspoon salt
- 1/4 cup white sugar
- 3 3/4 cups all-purpose flour
- 1 package active dry yeast
- Flour, for surface

DIRECTIONS:

1. Add all ingredients to the pan of your bread maker in the order listed above.
2. Set bread machine to Dough cycle. Once the Dough cycle is complete, roll dough out on a floured surface to about a 1-inch thickness.
3. Cut out 18 buns with a biscuit cutter or small glass and place them on a greased baking sheet.
4. Let buns rise about one hour or until they have doubled in size.
5. Bake at 350°F for 10 minutes.
6. Brush the tops of baked buns with melted butter and serve.

NUTRITIONAL INFO: CALORIES: 130, SODIUM: 118 MG, DIETARY Fiber: 0.8g, Fat: 2.2 g, Carbs: 23.7 g, Protein: 3.7 g.

Toasted Almond Whole Wheat Bread

An alternative to regular wheat bread, you can turn things up a notch with this delicious recipe. Toasted almond wheat bread is perfect for all your favorite meals. Excellent when toasted, top this bread with cream cheese and fruit for breakfast.

SERVINGS: 12 | PREP TIME: 10 MINUTES | COOK TIME: 3 HOURS

INGREDIENTS:

- 1 cup, plus 2 tablespoons water
- 3 tablespoons agave nectar
- 2 tablespoons butter, unsalted
- 1 1/2 cups bread flour
- 1 1/2 cups whole wheat flour
- 1/4 cup slivered almonds, toasted
- 1 teaspoon salt
- 1 1/2 teaspoons quick active dry yeast

DIRECTIONS:

1. Add all of the ingredients in bread machine pan in the order they appear above, reserving yeast.
2. Make a well in the center of the dry ingredients and add the yeast.
3. Select the Basic cycle, light or medium crust color, and press Start.
4. Remove baked bread from pan and cool on a rack before slicing.

NUTRITIONAL INFO: CALORIES: 150, SODIUM: 209 MG, DIETARY Fiber: 2.8 g, Fat: 3.4 g, Carbs: 26.5 g, Protein: 4.4 g.

Whole Wheat Rolls

For those who prefer the heartiness (and heart-healthiness) of whole wheat, this recipe for dinner rolls will satisfy that craving for soft, yummy bread to go with all your hot soups, stews and dishes!

SERVINGS: 12 | PREP TIME: 10 MINUTES | COOK TIME: 3 HOURS

INGREDIENTS:

- 1 tablespoon sugar
- 1 teaspoon salt
- 2 3/4 cups whole wheat flour
- 2 teaspoons dry active yeast
- 1/4 cup water
- 1 egg
- 7/8 cup milk
- 1/4 cup butter

DIRECTIONS:

1. All ingredients should be brought to room temperature before baking.
2. Add the wet ingredients to the bread maker pan.
3. Measure and add the dry ingredients (except yeast) to the pan.
4. Make a well in the center of the dry ingredients and add the yeast.
5. Carefully place the yeast in the hole.
6. Select the Dough cycle, then press Start.
7. Divide dough into 12 portions and shape them into balls.
8. Preheat an oven to 350°F. Place rolls on a greased baking pan.
9. Bake for 25 to 30 minutes, until golden brown.
10. Butter and serve warm.

NUTRITIONAL INFO: CALORIES: 147, SODIUM: 236 MG, DIETARY Fiber: 3.5 g, Fat: 5.1 g, Carbs: 22.1 g, Protein: 5.1 g.

Italian Restaurant Style Breadsticks

Whip up Italian restaurant-style breadsticks right in the comfort of your very own kitchen with this delicious recipe. Enjoy alongside soup and salad, or with your favorite Italian dish.

SERVINGS 12 - 16 | PREP TIME: 15 MINUTES | COOK TIME: 3 HOURS

INGREDIENTS:

- 1 1/2 cups warm water
- 2 tablespoons butter, unsalted and melted
- 4 1/4 cups bread flour
- 2 tablespoons sugar
- 1 tablespoon salt
- 1 package active dry yeast
- For the topping:
- 1 stick unsalted butter, melted
- 2 teaspoons garlic powder

- 1 teaspoons salt
- 1 teaspoon parsley

DIRECTIONS:

1. Add wet ingredients to your bread maker pan.
2. Mix dry ingredients, except yeast, and add to pan.
3. Make a well in the center of the dry ingredients and add the yeast.
4. Set to Dough cycle and press Start.
5. When the dough is done, roll out and cut into strips; keep in mind that they will double in size after they have risen, so roll them out thinner than a typical breadstick to yield room for them to grow.
6. Place on a greased baking sheet.
7. Cover the dough with a light towel and let sit in a warm area for 45 minutes to an hour.
8. Preheat an oven to 400°F.
9. Bake breadsticks for 6 to 7 minutes.
10. Mix the melted butter, garlic powder, salt and parsley in a small mixing bowl.
11. Brush the bread sticks with half the butter mixture; return to oven and bake for 5 to 8 additional minutes.
12. Remove breadsticks from the oven and brush the other half of the butter mixture.
13. Allow to cool for a few minutes before serving.

NUTRITIONAL INFO: CALORIES: 148, SODIUM: 450 MG, DIETARY Fiber: 1 g, Fat: 2.5 g, Carbs: 27.3 g, Protein: 3.7 g.

Bagels

Bagels are a delicious way to enjoy bread for breakfast and brunch! You can top these yummy bagels with your favorite traditional toppings like cream cheese, smoked salmon, butter, fruit spread, or even peanut butter.

SERVINGS: 9 | PREP TIME: 25 MINUTES | COOK TIME: 1 HOUR

INGREDIENTS:

- 1 cup warm water
- 1 1/2 teaspoons salt
- 2 tablespoons sugar
- 3 cups bread flour
- 2 1/4 teaspoons active dry yeast
- 3 quarts boiling water
- 3 tablespoons white sugar

- 1 tablespoon cornmeal
- 1 egg white
- Flour, for surface

DIRECTIONS:

1. Place in the bread machine pan in the following order: warm water, salt, sugar, and flour.
2. Make a well in the center of the dry ingredients and add the yeast.
3. Select Dough cycle and press Start.
4. When Dough cycle is complete, remove pan and let dough rest on a lightly floured surface. Stir 3 tablespoons of sugar into the boiling water.
5. Cut dough into 9 equal pieces and roll each piece into a small ball.
6. Flatten each ball with the palm of your hand. Poke a hole in the middle of each using your thumb. Twirl the dough on your finger to make the hole bigger, while evening out the dough around the hole.
7. Sprinkle an ungreased baking sheet with 1 teaspoon cornmeal. Place the bagel on the baking sheet and repeat until all bagels are formed.
8. Cover the shaped bagels with a clean kitchen towel and let rise for 10 minutes.
9. Preheat an oven to 375°F.
10. Carefully transfer the bagels, one by one, to the boiling water. Boil for 1 minute, turning halfway.
11. Drain on a clean towel. Arrange boiled bagels on the baking sheet.
12. Glaze the tops with egg white and sprinkle any toppings you desire.
13. Bake for 20 to 25 minutes or until golden brown.
14. Let cool on a wire rack before serving.

NUTRITIONAL INFO: CALORIES: 185, SODIUM: 394 MG, DIETARY Fiber: 1.4 g, Fat: 0.5 g, Carbs: 39.7 g, Protein: 5.2 g.

Friendship Bread

Friendship bread is an age-old tradition of passing bread starter amongst friends. You'll love this easy- to-make and versatile bread recipe that you can share with your loved ones, too!

SERVINGS: 12 | PREP TIME: 5 MINUTES | COOK TIME: 3 HOURS 10 MINUTES

INGREDIENTS:

- 1 cup Amish Friendship Bread Starter
- 3 eggs
- 2/3 cup vegetable oil
- 1/4 cup milk
- 1 cup sugar
- 1/2 teaspoon vanilla extract
- 2 teaspoons cinnamon
- 1 1/2 teaspoons baking powder
- 1/2 teaspoon salt

- 1/2 teaspoon baking soda
- 2 cups flour
- 2 small boxes instant vanilla pudding

DIRECTIONS:

1. Add all of the wet ingredients into the bread maker pan.
2. Add in dry ingredients, except sugar and cinnamon.
3. Set bread machine on Sweet cycle, light crust color and press Start.
4. During the last 30 minutes of baking, lift lid and quickly add 1/4 cup sugar and 1/4 teaspoon of cinnamon.
5. When finished baking, leave in bread machine for 20 minutes to rest.
6. Remove from baking pan and put loaf on a cooling rack.

NUTRITIONAL INFO: CALORIES: 379, SODIUM: 296 MG, DIETARY Fiber: 1.0 g, Fat: 13.7 g, Carbs: 61.25 g, Protein: 5.3 g.

Homemade Hot Dog and Hamburger Buns

When you want delicious hamburger and hot dog buns, why not make them at home? Gone are the days of bringing home smushed buns once you start whipping them up yourself with this delicious recipe!

SERVINGS: 8 - 10 | PREP TIME: 15 MINUTES | COOK TIME: 1 HOUR 35 MINUTES

INGREDIENTS:

- 1 1/4 cups milk, slightly warmed
- 1 egg, beaten
- 2 tablespoons butter, unsalted
- 1/4 cup white sugar
- 3/4 teaspoon salt
- 3 3/4 cups bread flour
- 1 1/4 teaspoons active dry yeast
- Flour, for surface

DIRECTIONS:

1. Place all ingredients into the pan of the bread maker in the following order, reserving yeast: milk, egg, butter, sugar, salt, flour.
2. Make a well in the center of the dry ingredients and add the yeast.
3. Select Dough cycle. When cycle is complete, turn out onto floured surface.
4. Cut dough in half and roll each half out to a 1" thick circle.
5. Cut each half into 6 (3 1/2") rounds with inverted glass as a cutter. (For hot dog buns, cut lengthwise into 1-inch-thick rolls, and cut a slit along the length of the bun for easier separation later.)
6. Place on a greased baking sheet far apart and brush with melted butter.
7. Cover and let rise until doubled, about one hour; preheat an oven to 350°F.
8. Bake for 9 minutes.
9. Let cool and serve with your favorite meats and toppings!

NUTRITIONAL INFO: CALORIES: 233, SODIUM: 212 MG, DIETARY Fiber: 1.4 g, Fat: 3.8 g, Carbs: 42.5 g, Protein: 6.6 g.

CAKES AND QUICK BREADS

Carrot Cake Bread

Sweet and savory carrots are the star of this delicious loaf of bread. Enjoy it warm with your favorite hot drink or drizzled with vanilla cream cheese icing.

SERVINGS: 12 - 16 | PREP TIME: 5 MINUTES | COOK TIME: 1 HOURS 20 MINUTES

INGREDIENTS:

- Non-stick cooking spray
- 1/4 cup vegetable oil
- 2 large eggs, room temperature
- 1/2 teaspoon pure vanilla extract
- 1/2 cup sugar
- 1/4 cup light brown sugar
- 1/4 cup crushed pineapple with juice (from can or fresh)
- 1 1/4 cups unbleached, all-purpose flour
- 1 teaspoon baking powder

- 1/4 teaspoon baking soda
- 1/4 teaspoon salt
- 1 teaspoon ground cloves
- 3/4 teaspoon ground cinnamon
- 1 cup freshly grated carrots
- 1/3 cup chopped pecans
- 1/3 cup golden raisins

DIRECTIONS:

1. Coat the inside of the bread pan with non-stick cooking spray.
2. Add all of the ingredients, in order listed, to the bread pan.
3. Select Express Bake, medium crust color, and press Start. While the batter is mixing, scrape the sides of the bread pan with a rubber spatula to fully incorporate ingredients.
4. When baked, remove from bread pan and place on wire rack to cool completely before slicing and serving.

NUTRITIONAL INFO: CALORIES: 151, SODIUM: 69 MG, DIETARY FIBER: 1.2 g, Fat: 7.2 g, Carbs: 20.1 g, Protein: 2.4 g.

Lemon Cake

Light and airy, this delicious lemon cake is perfect for anyone who loves citrus and sweet together. Drizzled with a sticky, sweet glaze, this is the perfect springtime dessert with a glass of sparkling water or sweet iced tea.

SERVINGS: 12 | PREP TIME: 5 MINUTES | COOK TIME: 2 HOURS 50 MINUTES

INGREDIENTS:

- 3 large eggs, beaten
- 1/3 cup 2% milk
- 1/2 cup butter, melted
- 2 cups all-purpose flour
- 3 teaspoons baking powder
- 1 1/3 cup sugar
- 1 teaspoon vanilla extract
- 2 lemons, zested

- For the glaze:
- 1 cup powdered sugar
- 2 tablespoons lemon juice, freshly squeezed

DIRECTIONS:

1. Prepare the glaze by whisking the powdered sugar and lemon juice together in a small mixing bowl and set aside.
2. Add all of the remaining ingredients to the baking pan in the order listed.
3. Select the Sweet bread, medium color crust, and press Start.
4. When baked, transfer the baking pan to a cooling rack.
5. When the cake has cooled completely, gently shake the cake out onto a serving plate. Glaze the cool cake and serve.

NUTRITIONAL INFO: CALORIES: 290, SODIUM: 77 MG, DIETARY Fiber: 0.6 g, Fat: 9.3 g, Carbs: 42.9 g, Protein: 4 g.

Insane Coffee Cake

Delicious coffee cake is insanely easy to make and that's what we love about this amazing recipe. Quick and yummy, we think you'll fall in love with it in no time. Make sure to serve a large slice with a hot cup of coffee for the full effect!

SERVINGS: 10 - 12 | PREP TIME: 15 MINUTES | COOK TIME: 2 HOURS

INGREDIENTS:

- 7/8 cup of milk
- 1/4 cup of sugar
- 1 teaspoon salt
- 1 egg yolk
- 1 tablespoon butter
- 2 1/4 cups bread flour
- 2 teaspoons of active dry yeast
- For the topping:

- 2 tablespoons butter, melted
- 2 tablespoons brown sugar
- 1 teaspoon cinnamon

DIRECTIONS:

1. Set the topping ingredients aside and add the rest of the ingredients to the bread pan in the order above.
2. Set the bread machine to the Dough cycle.
3. Butter a 9-by-9-inch glass baking dish and pour the dough into the dish. Cover with a towel and let rise for about 10 minutes.
4. Preheat an oven to 375°F.
5. Brush the dough with the melted butter.
6. Mix the brown sugar and cinnamon in a bowl and sprinkle on top of the coffee cake.
7. Let the topped dough rise, uncovered, for another 30 minutes.
8. Place in oven and bake for 30 to 35 minutes or until a wooden toothpick inserted into the center comes out clean and dry.
9. When baked, let the coffee cake rest for 10 minutes. Carefully remove the coffee cake from the dish with a rubber spatula, slice and serve.

NUTRITIONAL INFO: CALORIES: 148, SODIUM: 211 MG, DIETARY Fiber: 0.9 g, Fat: 3.9 g, Carbs: 24.9 g, Protein: 3.5 g.

Chocolate Marble Cake

Chocolate lovers will fall head over heels for this scrumptious cake. Marbled cake is absolutely beautiful and decadent when served for brunch or for a ladies luncheon with tea and coffee.

SERVINGS: 12 - 16 | PREP TIME: 15 MINUTES | COOK TIME: 3 HOURS 45 MINUTES

INGREDIENTS:

- 1 1/2 cups water
- 1 1/2 teaspoons vanilla extract
- 1 1/2 teaspoons salt
- 3 1/2 cups bread flour
- 1 1/2 teaspoons instant yeast
- 1 cup semi-sweet chocolate chips

DIRECTIONS:

1. Set the chocolate chips aside and add the other ingredients to the pan of your bread maker.
2. Program the machine for Sweet bread and press Start.
3. Check the dough after 10 to 15 minutes of kneading; you should have a smooth ball, soft but not sticky.
4. Add the chocolate chips about 3 minutes before the end of the second kneading cycle.
5. Once baked, remove with a rubber spatula and allow to cool on a rack before serving.

NUTRITIONAL INFO: CALORIES: 172, SODIUM: 218 MG, DIETARY Fiber: 1.6 g, Fat: 4.3 g, Carbs: 30.1 g, Protein: 3 g.

Lemon Blueberry Quick Bread

❧❀❧

Light and airy, this scrumptious quick bread is packed full of bright blueberries. Perfect for any brunch or birthday lunch, you'll love making this yummy dessert.

SERVINGS: 10 - 12 | PREP TIME: 20 MINUTES | COOK TIME: 2 HOURS

INGREDIENTS:

- 2 cups all-purpose flour
- 1 1/2 teaspoons baking powder
- 1/2 teaspoon salt
- 1 tablespoon lemon zest
- 1 cup sugar
- 1/2 cup unsalted butter, softened
- 2 large eggs
- 2 teaspoons pure vanilla extract
- 1/2 cup whole milk

- 1 1/2 cups blueberries
- For the crumb topping:
- 1/3 cup sugar
- 3 tablespoons all-purpose flour
- 2 tablespoons butter, melted
- Non-stick cooking spray

DIRECTIONS:

1. Spray bread maker pan with non-stick cooking spray and lightly flour.
2. Combine crumb topping ingredients and set aside.
3. In a small bowl, whisk together flour, baking powder and salt and set aside.
4. In a large mixing bowl, combine sugar and lemon zest. Add butter and beat until light and fluffy. Add eggs, vanilla and milk.
5. Add flour mixture and mix just until combine. Stir in blueberries and spread batter evenly into bread maker pan.
6. Top with crumb topping; select Sweet bread, light color crust, and press Start.
7. When done cool on a wire rack for 15 minutes and serve warm.

NUTRITIONAL INFO: CALORIES: 462, SODIUM: 332 MG, DIETARY Fiber: 1 g, Fat: 32.1 g, Carbs: 41.8 g, Protein: 4 g.

Cinnamon Pecan Coffee Cake

Cinnamon pecan boffee cake is a decadent way to serve up a sweet treat for friends and co-workers. This delicious recipe will also fill your home with a delightful bakery-sweet smell.

SERVINGS: 10 - 12 | PREP TIME: 15 MINUTES | COOK TIME: 2 HOURS

INGREDIENTS:

- 1 cup butter, unsalted
- 1 cup sugar
- 2 eggs
- 1 cup sour cream
- 1 teaspoon vanilla extract
- 2 cups all-purpose flour
- 1 teaspoon baking powder
- 1 teaspoon baking soda
- 1/2 teaspoon salt

- For the topping:
- 1/2 cup brown sugar
- 1/4 cup sugar
- 1/2 teaspoon cinnamon
- 1/2 cup pecans, chopped

DIRECTIONS:

1. Add butter, sugar, eggs, sour cream and vanilla to the bread maker baking pan, followed by the dry ingredients.
2. Select Cake cycle and press Start.
3. Prepare topping and set aside.
4. When kneading cycle is done, after about 20 minutes, sprinkle 1/2 cup of topping on top of dough and continue baking.
5. During the last hour of baking time, sprinkle the remaining 1/2 cup of topping on the cake. Bake until complete. Cool on a wire rack for 10 minutes and serve warm.

NUTRITIONAL INFO: CALORIES: 488, SODIUM: 333 MG, DIETARY Fiber: 2.5 g, Fat: 32.8 g, Carbs: 46.4 g, Protein: 5.7 g.

King Cake

Bake up something special for Mardi Gras with a taste of New Orleans. This traditional King Cake recipe will have everyone wanting to be "king for the day"!

SERVINGS: 12 - 16 | PREP TIME: 25 MINUTES | COOK TIME: 2 HOURS 55 MINUTES

INGREDIENTS:

For the Dough:

- 1 egg, lightly beaten
- 1/4 cup filtered water
- 1/2 teaspoon salt
- 2 tablespoons unsalted butter, room temperature
- 1 cup sour cream
- 3 1/2 tablespoons sugar
- 3 1/2 cups all-purpose flour
- 2 1/2 teaspoons bread machine yeast

For the Filling:

- 1 cup cream cheese, room temperature
- 1/2 cup confectioners' sugar
- 1/2 cup sugar
- 2 teaspoons ground cinnamon
- 5 tablespoons unsalted butter, melted
- For the Icing:
- 1/2 cup cream cheese, room temperature
- 1/4 cup unsalted butter, room temperature
- 2 1/2 cups confectioners' sugar
- 1 teaspoon pure vanilla extract
- Purple, green, and yellow cake glitter
- Flour, for surface

DIRECTIONS:

1. Add the dough ingredients to the bread machine in the order listed.
2. Select Dough cycle, and press Start.
3. Check the dough after five minutes of mixing and add 1 to 2 more tablespoons of water or flour if the dough is too dry or too wet.
4. In a large mixing bowl, beat the cream cheese and 1/2 cup confectioners' sugar until smooth; set aside. Mix 1/2 cup sugar, 2 teaspoons cinnamon, and 5 tablespoons melted butter until combined; set aside.
5. Line a large baking sheet with parchment paper and set aside.
6. Remove the dough and roll out into a 10-by-28-inch rectangle on a floured surface. Trim the edges as needed with scissors.
7. Spread the cream cheese mixture on the dough to within 1 inch of the edges.

8. Spread sugar-cinnamon mixture on the cream cheese to within 1 inch of the edges of the dough.

9. Starting at one of the long edges, roll the dough tightly into a log. Pinch the edges to seal the log and place the rolled dough onto the lined baking sheet, seam side down, and form the dough into a ring.

10. Moisten the ends of the dough with a little water and pinch the two ends together to seal. Place a large greased can in the center to maintain a nice circle in the center. Cover with a towel and let rise in a warm place until doubled in size, about 30 minutes.

11. Preheat oven to 350°F. Bake the cake until the top is golden brown, about 25 minutes.

12. Mix the ingredients for the icing until just smooth in a mixing bowl.

13. Remove the cake from the oven and allow to cool for 10 minutes on a wire rack.

14. While the cake is still warm, spoon the icing onto the cake and sprinkle with purple, green and yellow glitter.

NUTRITIONAL INFO: CALORIES: 383, SODIUM: 205 MG, DIETARY Fiber: 1 g, Fat: 18.9 g, Carbs: 48.5 g, Protein: 5.6 g.

Honey Pound Cake

Sweet treats are just as easy to whip up in your bread maker as a loaf of crusty bread. Just be sure to follow the directions and you'll get perfect cake every time!

SERVINGS: 12 - 16 | PREP TIME: 5 MINUTES | COOK TIME: 2 HOURS 50 MINUTES

INGREDIENTS:

- 1 cup butter, unsalted
- 1/4 cup honey
- 2 tablespoons whole milk
- 4 eggs, beaten
- 1 cup sugar
- 2 cups flour

DIRECTIONS:

1. Bring the butter to room temperature and cut into 1/2-inch cubes.
2. Add the ingredients to the bread machine in the order listed (butter, honey, milk, eggs, sugar, flour).
3. Press Sweet bread setting, light crust color, and press Start.
4. Take the cake out of the bread pan using a rubber spatula, as soon as it's finished. Cool on a rack and serve with your favorite fruit.

NUTRITIONAL INFO: CALORIES: 117, SODIUM: 183 MG, DIETARY Fiber: 0.3 g, Fat: 6.9 g, Carbs: 12.3 g, Protein: 1.9 g.

German Butter Cake

A classic, old world-style cake that you will love serving to the whole family. Perfect for afternoon coffee, this cake will also impress your guests with its delicate flavor!

SERVINGS: 12 - 16 | PREP TIME: 10 MINUTES | COOK TIME: 2 HOUR 25 MINUTES

INGREDIENTS:

- 2 teaspoons active dry yeast
- 1/4 cup sugar
- 2 1/4 cups all-purpose flour
- 1 teaspoon salt
- 7/8 cup whole milk, lukewarm
- 1 egg yolk
- 1 tablespoon butter, softened
- For the topping:
- 3 tablespoons butter, cold

- 1/2 cup almonds, sliced
- 1/3 cup sugar

DIRECTIONS:

1. Add all of the dough ingredients to the bread maker pan.
2. Press Dough cycle and Start.
3. Grease a 10-inch springform pan; when the dough cycle is finished, pat the dough into the pan.
4. Prepare the topping by cutting the butter into - inch squares and place them sporadically over the surface of the dough, slightly pushing each into the dough.
5. Sprinkle with almond slices, then sprinkle evenly with sugar.
6. Cover with a towel and let stand in a warm place for 30 minutes.
7. Preheat an oven to 375 ° F.
8. Bake for 20 to 25 minutes or until golden brown.
9. Let cool 10 minutes in pan on cooling rack and serve warm!

NUTRITIONAL INFO: CALORIES: 226, SODIUM: 228 MG, DIETARY Fiber: 1 g, Fat: 9.1 g, Carbs: 29.8 g, Protein: 7.1 g.

Donuts

Sugary, soft donuts can be baked right in the comfort of your kitchen with this yummy bread maker donut recipe. Transform your house into a sweet little bakery when you whip them up in your very own bread maker.

SERVINGS: 24 | PREP TIME: 25 MINUTES | COOK TIME: 55 MINUTES

INGREDIENTS:

- 1 1/4 cups whole milk
- 1 beaten egg
- 1/4 cup shortening
- 1/4 cup sugar
- 1 teaspoon salt
- 3 1/2 cups all-purpose flour
- 1 1/2 teaspoons dry yeast

DIRECTIONS:

1. Measure ingredients into the bread maker, first adding wet then dry ingredients as listed above, reserving yeast.
2. Make a well in the flour; pour the yeast into the hole.
3. Select Dough cycle and press Start.
4. Roll kneaded dough out to a 1/2-inch thick rectangle and cut with a 2 1/2 inch donut cutter.
5. Let rise, covered, for 30 minutes or until doubled in size.
6. Preheat a deep fryer to 375°F.
7. Drop donuts into fryer and turn donuts as they rise to the surface. Fry until golden brown.
8. Drain on paper towels to cool. Glaze or dust with your favorite donut topping while warm and serve.

NUTRITIONAL INFO: CALORIES: 104, SODIUM: 105 MG, DIETARY Fiber: 0.5 g, Fat: 3 g, Carbs: 16.7 g, Protein: 2.7 g.

Chocolate Chip Bread

Chocolate lovers will fall head over heels for this loaf of bread. This is one delicious chocolate-laced dessert you can whip up in no time.

SERVINGS: 15 | PREP TIME: 5 MINUTES | COOK TIME: 3 HOURS

INGREDIENTS:

- 1/4 cup water
- 1 cup milk
- 1 egg
- 3 cups bread flour
- 3 tablespoons brown sugar
- 2 tablespoons white sugar
- 1 teaspoon salt
- 1 teaspoon ground cinnamon
- 1 1/2 teaspoons active dry yeast
- 2 tablespoons butter, softened

DIRECTIONS:

1. Place ingredients in the pan of the bread maker in the order listed above.
2. Select Sweet bread cycle and press Start.
3. Add the chocolate chips about 5 minutes before the kneading cycle has finished.
4. Remove loaf from bread maker pan to cool on a wire rack when bake cycle finishes. Serve with milk or your favorite hot drink!

NUTRITIONAL INFO: CALORIES: 131, SODIUM: 179, DIETARY FIBER: 0.8 g, Fat: 2.4 g, Carbs: 23.5 g, Protein: 3.7 g.

Rainbow Swirl Cake

Rainbow swirls make this cake absolutely magical! Ice this luscious dessert with fondant or buttercream icing to make a truly decadent birthday cake or party cake with this yummy recipe.

SERVINGS: 15 | PREP TIME: 35 MINUTES | COOK TIME: 3 HOURS

INGREDIENTS:

- 1 cup milk plus 1 egg yolk
- 3 cups unbleached all-purpose flour
- 2 1/2 tablespoons sugar
- 2 1/4 teaspoons active dry yeast
- 1 1/2 tablespoons unsalted butter, softened
- 2 teaspoons salt
- Red, yellow, green and blue food coloring
- Flour, for surface

DIRECTIONS:

1. Whisk milk and egg yolk together in a microwave safe bowl and microwave 30 seconds; add to bread maker pan.
2. Whisk together flour, sugar and yeast in a large mixing bowl and add to bread maker pan.
3. Add milk mixture, butter, salt, and stir to combine; add to bread maker pan.
4. Select Dough cycle and press Start.
5. When kneading is finished, divide dough into 5 equal dough balls and place each one in a small bowl and cover with a tea towel.
6. Remove one piece from a bowl and place it on a plastic cutting board. Add several drops of food coloring and knead the food coloring into the dough with gloved hands, adding more food coloring until it is fully incorporated.
7. Shape dough into a ball and return to its bowl. Repeat with remaining pieces of dough, dying each a different color; be sure to wash your hands and your work surface between each color.
8. Cover each bowl with plastic wrap and let rise until doubled; about 2 hours.
9. Punch down each dough ball when risen.
10. Roll the red dough ball out on a lightly floured surface into an 8-by-4-inch rectangle. Roll out yellow piece of dough into an 8-by-4-inch rectangle and place directly on top of the red dough. Repeat with green, blue, and purple dough balls until you have a stack of 8-by-4-inch rectangles.
11. Roll up dough tightly from the short end into a loaf.
12. Place loaf in a lightly greased 9-by-5-inch loaf pan. Cover with a tea towel or plastic wrap and let rise until doubled, about 1 hour.
13. Preheat oven to 375°F and bake until browned on top and a

thermometer inserted in the bottom center reads 190° F, about 30 minutes.

14. Remove loaf from pan and cool completely on a wirerack before slicing.

NUTRITIONAL INFO: CALORIES: 122, SODIUM: 327 MG, DIETARY Fiber: 0.8 g, Fat: 2.1 g, Carbs: 22.2 g, Protein: 3.5 g.

Pumpkin Spice Cake

For the pumpkin spice lover at heart, this delicious cake is easy to make in your bread maker. Serve on a cool fall day with your favorite hot drinks!

SERVINGS: 12 | PREP TIME: 5 MINUTES | COOK TIME: 2 HOURS 50 MINUTES

INGREDIENTS:

- 1 cup sugar
- 1 cup canned pumpkin
- 1/3 cup vegetable oil
- 1 teaspoon vanilla extract
- 2 eggs
- 1 1/2 cups all-purpose flour
- 2 teaspoons baking powder
- 1/4 teaspoon salt
- 1 teaspoon ground cinnamon

- 1/4 teaspoon ground nutmeg
- 1/8 teaspoon ground cloves
- Shortening, for greasing pan

DIRECTIONS:

1. Grease bread maker pan and kneading blade generously with shortening.
2. Add all ingredients to the bread maker pan in the order listed above.
3. Select Rapid cycle and press Start.
4. Open the lid three minutes into the cycle and carefully scrape down sides of pan with a rubber spatula; close lid to continue cycle.
5. Cool baked cake for 10 minutes on a wire rack before slicing.

NUTRITIONAL INFO: CALORIES: 195, SODIUM: 64 MG, DIETARY Fiber: 1.3 g, Fat: 7.1 g, Carbs: 31.2 g, Protein: 2.8 g.

Peanut Butter Bread

Peanut butter is the star of this rich, decadent loaf of bread. Eat as-is, or spread jam or honey on a slice and serve it with a glass of milk for a protein-packed snack.

SERVINGS: 12 | PREP TIME: 5 MINUTES | COOK TIME: 3 HOURS

INGREDIENTS:

- 1 1/4 cups water
- 1/4 cup brown sugar
- 1/2 teaspoon salt
- 1/2 cup peanut butter
- 3 cups bread flour
- 3 teaspoons active dry yeast
- For the topping:
- 1 tablespoon creamy peanut butter
- 2/3 cup powdered sugar

- 4 teaspoons water

DIRECTIONS:

1. Layer the ingredients (except yeast) in the bread machine pan in the order listed above.
2. Make a well in the center of the dry ingredients and add the yeast.
3. Select Basic bread setting, light color crust, and press Start.
4. Transfer bread to a cooling rack.
5. Combine topping ingredients and drizzle over the bread.
6. Allow to cool and serve.

NUTRITIONAL INFO: CALORIES: 217 SODIUM: 148 MG, DIETARY Fiber: 1.7 g, Fat: 5.8 g, Carbs: 36 g, Protein: 6.3 g.

Apple Raisin Nut Cake

The sweetness of apples and raisins come together with savory nuts to make a delicious cake in this Apple Raisin Nut Cake. Serve it up as an after-dinner treat.

SERVINGS: 10 | PREP TIME: 5 MINUTES | COOK TIME: 45 MINUTES

INGREDIENTS:

- 2 large eggs, lightly beaten
- 1/4 cup milk
- 1/3 cup butter, melted
- 1 1/2 cups all-purpose flour
- 3 teaspoons baking powder
- 1/4 cup sugar
- 1/4 teaspoon salt
- 1 teaspoon cinnamon
- 1 teaspoon pure vanilla extract

- Add after the kneading process:
- 1 small apple, peeled and roughly chopped
- 1/4 cup raisins
- 1/4 cup walnuts, chopped
- 1 teaspoon all-purpose flour

DIRECTIONS:

1. Add ingredients in the order listed above.
2. Press Sweet cycle, light color crust, and Start.
3. Mix apples, raisins, walnuts, and flour together in a small mixing bowl. Add to dough after the kneading process.
4. Allow to cool on a cooling rack for 15 minutes before serving.

NUTRITIONAL INFO: CALORIES: 204, SODIUM: 121 MG, DIETARY Fiber: 1.5 g, Fat: 9.4 g, Carbs: 26.9 g, Protein: 4.4 g.

SAVORY BREADS

10 Minute Rosemary Bread

While you can't have a fresh loaf of bread in 10 minutes, you can prep bread in just 10 minutes with this recipe - and you'll get fresh-baked bread in half the time of a traditional loaf. Seasoned with aromatic rosemary, this bread is delicious served alongside savory
dishes and cheese.

SERVINGS: 12 | PREP TIME: 15 MINUTES | COOK TIME: 2 HOURS

INGREDIENTS:

- 1 cup warm water, about 105°F
- 2 tablespoons butter, softened
- 1 egg
- 3 cups all-purpose flour
- 1/4 cup whole wheat flour
- 1/3 cup sugar
- 1 teaspoon salt

- 3 teaspoons bread maker yeast
- 2 tablespoons rosemary, freshly chopped
- For the topping:
- 1 egg, room temperature
- 1 teaspoon milk, room temperature
- Garlic powder
- Sea salt

DIRECTIONS:

1. Place all of the ingredients in the bread maker pan in the order listed above.
2. Select Dough cycle.
3. When dough is kneaded, place on parchment paper on a flat surface and roll into two loaves; set aside and allow to rise for 30 minutes.
4. Preheat a pizza stone in an oven on 375°F for 30 minutes.
5. For the topping, add the egg and milk to a small mixing bowl and whisk to create an egg wash. Baste the formed loaves and sprinkle evenly with garlic powder and sea salt.
6. Allow to rise for 40 minutes, lightly covered, in a warm area.
7. Bake for 15 to 18 minutes or until golden brown. Serve warm.

NUTRITIONAL INFO: CALORIES: 176, SODIUM: 220 MG, DIETARY Fiber: 1.5 g, Fat: 3.1 g, Carbs: 32 g, Protein: 5 g.

Garlic Cheese Pull-Apart Rolls

Garlic and cheese come together to make these rolls irresistible! Even the kids will love this pull-apart bread served alongside spaghetti or ravioli.

SERVINGS: 12 - 24 | PREP TIME: 20 MINUTES | COOK TIME: 3 HOURS

INGREDIENTS:

- 1 cup water
- 3 cups bread flour
- 1 1/2 teaspoons salt
- 1-1/2 tablespoons butter
- 3 tablespoons sugar
- 2 tablespoons nonfat dry milk powder
- 2 teaspoons yeast
- For the topping:
- 1/4 cup butter, melted

- 1 garlic clove, crushed
- 2 tablespoons parmesan cheese, plus more if needed
- Flour, for surface

DIRECTIONS:

1. Place first 6 ingredients in bread maker pan in order listed.
2. Make a well in the flour; pour the yeast into the hole.
3. Select Dough cycle, press Start.
4. Turn finished dough onto a floured countertop.
5. Gently roll and stretch dough into a 24-inch rope.
6. Grease a 13-by-9-inch baking sheet.
7. Divide dough into 24 pieces with a sharp knife and shape into balls; place on prepared pan. Combine butter and garlic in a small mixing bowl and pour over rolls.
8. Sprinkle rolls evenly with parmesan cheese.
9. Cover and let rise for 30-45 minutes until doubled.
10. Bake at 375°F for 10 to 15 minutes or until golden brown.
11. Remove from oven, pull apart, and serve warm.

NUTRITIONAL INFO: CALORIES: 109, SODIUM: 210 MG, DIETARY Fiber: 0.6 g, Fat: 3.5 g, Carbs: 16.7 g, Protein: 2.6 g.

Craft Beer and Cheese Bread

Hoppy beer and delicious cheese come together to make this gorgeous loaf that everyone in your family will love. Serve it at a tailgate or party with your favorite dips and spreads. Try different cheese combinations for different flavor fun.

SERVINGS: 10 | PREP TIME: 10 MINUTES | COOK TIME: 2 HOURS 10 MINUTES

INGREDIENTS:

- 1 package active dry yeast
- 3 cups all-purpose flour
- 1 tablespoon sugar
- 1 1/2 teaspoons salt
- 1 tablespoon butter, room temperature
- 1 1/4 cups craft beer, at room temperature
- 1/2 cup cheddar cheese, shredded
- 1/2 cup Monterey Jack cheese, shredded

DIRECTIONS:

1. Add beer to a sauce pan with cheese and heat on low until just warm; stir to blend.
2. Transfer mixture to the bread maker pan.
3. Measure and add dry ingredients (except yeast) to the bread pan. Make a small "hole" in the flour for the yeast.
4. Carefully pour the yeast into the "hole."
5. Snap the baking pan into the bread maker and close the lid.
6. Choose the Basic setting and preferred crust color and press Start.
7. When the loaf is done, remove the pan from the machine. After about 5 minutes, gently shake the pan to loosen the loaf and turn it out onto a rack to cool.
8. Serve warm.

NUTRITIONAL INFO: CALORIES: 209, SODIUM: 425 MG, DIETARY Fiber: 1.2 g, Fat: 5.1 g, Carbs: 31.2 g, Protein: 7.1 g.

Blue Cheese Bread

Gooey blue cheese bread is sure to warm your cheese-loving soul when you bake up this delicious loaf. Serve this tangy bread on its own or alongside your favorite soup for one hearty meal.

SERVINGS: 10 - 12 | PREP TIME: 5 MINUTES | COOK TIME: 3 HOURS

INGREDIENTS:

- 3/4 cup warm water
- 1 large egg
- 1 teaspoon salt
- 3 cups bread flour
- 1 cup blue cheese, crumbled
- 2 tablespoons nonfat dry milk
- 2 tablespoons sugar
- 1 teaspoon bread machine yeast

DIRECTIONS:

1. Add the ingredients to bread machine pan in the order listed above, (except yeast) ; be sure to add the cheese with the flour.
2. Make a well in the flour; pour the yeast into the hole.
3. Select Basic bread cycle, medium crust color, and press Start.
4. When finished, transfer to a cooling rack for 10 minutes and serve warm.

NUTRITIONAL INFO: CALORIES: 171, SODIUM: 266 MG, DIETARY Fiber: 0.9 g, Fat: 3.9 g, Carbs: 26.8 g, Protein: 6.7 g.

Savory Bread Maker Rolls

Savory Bread Maker Rolls are easy to prepare and have a rich, satisfying taste! Perfect to serve with salads, soups, or just on their own with a slice of cheese.

SERVINGS: 24 | PREP TIME: 25 MINUTES | COOK TIME: 2 HOURS 10 MINS

INGREDIENTS:

- 1 cup warm milk, 70° to 80°F
- 1/2 cup butter, softened
- 1/4 cup sugar
- 2 eggs
- 1 1/2 teaspoons salt
- 4 cups bread flour
- 2 tablespoons herbes de Provence
- 2 1/4 teaspoons active dry yeast
- Flour, for surface

DIRECTIONS:

1. Add all ingredients in the order listed above to the bread maker pan, reserving yeast.
2. Make a well in the flour; add yeast to the hole.
3. Select Dough setting; when Dough cycle is completed, turn dough out onto a lightly floured surface.
4. Divide dough into 24 portions and shape into balls.
5. Place rolls in a greased 13-by-9-inch baking pan.
6. Cover and let rise in a warm place for 30-45 minutes; preheat an oven to 350°F.
7. Bake for 13-16 minutes or until golden brown and serve warm.

NUTRITIONAL INFO: CALORIES: 129, SODIUM: 185 MG, DIETARY Fiber: 0.6 g, Fat: 4.6 g, Carbs: 18.7 g, Protein: 3.1 g.

Pepperoni Bread

Whip up a savory treat the whole family will love when you bake your very own pepperoni bread in your bread maker. Serve with your favorite Italian dish or on its own with pizza dipping sauce.

SERVINGS: 10 | PREP TIME: 5 MINUTES | COOK TIME: 3 HOURS 10 MINUTES

INGREDIENTS:

- 1 cup plus 2 tablespoons warm water
- 1/3 cup mozzarella cheese, shredded
- 2 tablespoons sugar
- 1 1/2 teaspoons garlic salt
- 1 1/2 teaspoons dried oregano
- 3 1/4 cups bread flour
- 1 1/2 teaspoons active dry yeast
- 2/3 cup sliced pepperoni

DIRECTIONS:

1. Add the first six ingredients in order listed above, reserving the yeast.
2. Make a well in the flour; pour the yeast into the hole.
3. Select Basic bread setting, medium crust color, and press Start.
4. Check dough after 5 minutes of mixing and add 1 to 2 tablespoons of water or flour if needed. Just before the final kneading, add the pepperoni.
5. Remove loaf when finished and allow to cool for 10 to 15 minutes on a cooling rack before serving.

NUTRITIONAL INFO: CALORIES: 165, SODIUM: 13 MG, DIETARY FIBER: 1.4 g, Fat: 0.8 g, Carbs: 34.1 g, Protein: 4.9 g.

Golden Turmeric Cardamom Bread

With a lovely golden color and a fragrant cardamom flavor, you will love serving this bread with savory, spicy or sweet dishes. Great with a dab of butter and honey.

SERVINGS: 12 | PREP TIME: 5 MINUTES | COOK TIME: 3 HOURS

INGREDIENTS:

- 1 cup lukewarm water
- 1/3 cup lukewarm milk
- 3 tablespoons butter, unsalted
- 3 3/4 cups unbleached all-purpose flour
- 3 tablespoons sugar
- 1 1/2 teaspoons salt
- 2 tablespoons ground turmeric
- 1 tablespoon ground cardamom
- 1/2 teaspoon cayenne pepper

- 1 1/2 teaspoons active dry yeast

DIRECTIONS:

1. Add liquid ingredients to the bread pan.
2. Measure and add dry ingredients (except yeast) to the bread pan.
3. Make a well in the center of the dry ingredients and add the yeast.
4. Snap the baking pan into the bread maker and close the lid.
5. Choose the Basic setting, preferred crust color and press Start.
6. When the loaf is done, remove the pan from the machine. After about 5 minutes, gently shake the pan to loosen the loaf and turn it out onto a rack to cool.

NUTRITIONAL INFO: CALORIES: 183, SODIUM: 316 MG, DIETARY Fiber: 1.2 g, Fat: 3.3 g, Carbs: 33.3 g, Protein: 4.5 g.

Prosciutto Parmesan Breadsticks

Delicate prosciutto and robust parmesan cheese make these breadsticks simply to die for! You'll love serving these warm treats at your next holiday party when you need something a little fancier than basic bread sticks.

SERVINGS: 12 | PREP TIME: 15 MINUTES | COOK TIME: 2 HOURS 10 MINUTES

INGREDIENTS:

- 1 1/3 cups warm water
- 1 tablespoon butter
- 1 1/2 tablespoons sugar
- 1 1/2 teaspoons salt
- 4 cups bread flour
- 2 teaspoons yeast
- For the topping:
- 1/2 pound prosciutto, sliced very thin

- 1/2 cup of grated parmesan cheese
- 1 egg yolk
- 1 tablespoon of water

DIRECTIONS:

1. Place the first set of dough ingredients (except yeast) in the bread pan in the order indicated. Do not add any of the topping ingredients yet.
2. Make a well in the center of the dry ingredients and add the yeast.
3. Select the Dough cycle on the bread machine. When finished, drop the dough onto a lightly-floured surface.
4. Roll the dough out flat to about 1/4-inch thick, or about half a centimeter. Cover with plastic wrap and let rise for 20 to 30 minutes.
5. Sprinkle dough evenly with parmesan and carefully lay the prosciutto slices on the surface of the dough to cover as much of it as possible.
6. Preheat an oven to 400°F.
7. Cut the dough into 12 long strips, about one inch wide. Twist each end in opposite directions, twisting the toppings into the bread stick.
8. Place the breadsticks onto a lightly greased baking sheet.
9. Whisk the egg yolk and water together in a small mixing bowl and lightly baste each breadstick.
10. Bake for 8 to 10 minutes or until golden brown.
11. Remove from oven and serve warm.

NUTRITIONAL INFO: CALORIES: 207, SODIUM: 548 MG, DIETARY Fiber: 1.3 g, Fat: 3.3 g, Carbs: 34 g, Protein: 9.5 g.

Onion Loaf

Warm Onion Loaf is just the way to kick things up a notch with homemade dips like spinach and artichoke. You'll also love this bread served with tomato soup or a hearty vegetable soup.

SERVINGS: 12 | PREP TIME: 15 MINUTES | COOK TIME: 3 HOURS 40 MINUTES

INGREDIENTS:
- 1 tablespoon butter
- 2 medium onions, sliced
- 1 cup water
- 1 tablespoon olive or vegetable oil
- 3 cups bread flour
- 2 tablespoons sugar
- 1 teaspoon salt
- 1 1/4 teaspoons bread machine or quick active dry yeast

DIRECTIONS:
1. Preheat a large skillet to medium-low heat and add butter to

melt. Add onions and cook for 10 to 15 minutes, stirring often, until onions are brown and caramelized; remove from heat.

2. Add remaining ingredients, except onions, to the bread maker pan in the order listed above.

3. Select the Basic cycle, medium crust color, and press Start.

4. Add 1/2 cup of the onions 5 to 10 minutes before the last kneading cycle ends.

5. Remove baked bread from pan and allow to cool on a cooling rack before serving.

Nutritional Info: Calories: 149, Sodium: 203 mg, Dietary Fiber: 1.3 g, Fat: 2.5 g, Carbs: 27.7 g, Protein: 3.7 g.

Olive Loaf

A dense, robust loaf of bread, olive loaf goes well with just a pat of butter, or olive oil for dipping. Perfect for creamy soups and vinaigrette-dressed salads, this loaf is sure to become a dinner favorite.

SERVINGS: 12 | PREP TIME: 5 MINUTES | COOK TIME: 4 HOURS

INGREDIENTS:

- 1 cup plus 2 tablespoons water
- 1 tablespoon olive oil
- 3 cups bread flour
- 2 tablespoons instant nonfat dry milk
- 1 tablespoon sugar
- 1 1/4 teaspoons salt
- 1/4 teaspoon garlic powder
- 2 teaspoons active dry yeast
- 2/3 cup grated parmesan cheese

- 1 cup pitted Greek olives, sliced and drained

DIRECTIONS:

1. Add ingredients, except yeast, olives and cheese, to bread maker in order listed above.
2. Make a well in the flour; pour the yeast into the hole.
3. Select Basic cycle, light crust color, and press Start; do not use delay cycle.
4. Just before the final kneading, add the olives and cheese.
5. Remove and allow to cool on a wire rack for 15 minutes before serving.

NUTRITIONAL INFO: CALORIES: 149, SODIUM: 331 MG, DIETARY Fiber: 0.9 g, Fat: 2.8 g, Carbs: 25.5 g, Protein: 4.9 g.

Everything Bagel Loaf

If you love "everything" bagels, this yummy recipe will really hit the spot. Serve it toasted with cream cheese or topped with chicken salad for a fun lunch.

SERVINGS: 6 - 8 | PREP TIME: 5 MINUTES | COOK TIME: 3 HOURS 25 MINUTES

INGREDIENTS:

- 1 cup plus 3 tablespoons water
- 2 tablespoons vegetable oil
- 1 1/2 teaspoons salt
- 2 tablespoons sugar
- 3 1/4 cups white bread flour
- 3 tablespoons Everything Bagel seasoning
- 2 teaspoons active dry yeast

DIRECTIONS:

1. Add water and oil to the bread maker pan.
2. Add salt, Everything Bagel seasoning, and sugar.
3. Add flour.
4. Make a small well on top of the flour and be sure it does not reach wet ingredients. Add the yeast to the well.
5. Select Basic bread cycle, medium crust color, and press Start.
6. When bread is baked, allow the loaf cool on a cooling rack for about 30 minutes before serving.

NUTRITIONAL INFO: CALORIES: 44, SODIUM: 438 MG, DIETARY Fiber: 0.2 g, Fat: 3.5 g, Carbs: 3.4 g, Protein: 0.4 g.

Pizza Rolls

You'll simply fall in love with these delicious pizza rolls stuffed with cheese and sauce. While the recipe calls for my favorite toppings, don't be afraid to use what you want in the same measurements as below.

SERVINGS: 15 | PREP TIME: 25 MINUTES | COOK TIME: 3 HOURS

INGREDIENTS:

- 1 cup warm water
- 3 tablespoons olive oil
- 3 cups bread flour
- 3 tablespoons sugar
- 1 1/2 teaspoons salt
- 2 1/4 teaspoons instant yeast
- For the Filling:
- 1 package pepperoni, sliced

- 1 bag mozzarella cheese, shredded
- 1 cup pizza sauce
- 1 jar of mild banana pepper rings

DIRECTIONS:

1. Add the liquid ingredients to your bread maker first, then add flour and salt.
2. Create a small hole in the flour and add the sugar and yeast.
3. Select the Dough cycle and press Start.
4. Once your dough has fully risen, lay it out on a lightly floured surface, and punch it back down.
5. Knead by hand for about 30 seconds; be sure not to overwork the dough.
6. Pinch off a small amount of dough and flatten out into the shape of a circle and baste with one teaspoon of sauce. Layer with three slices of pepperoni, a good pinch of cheese, and a few banana pepper rings.
7. Fold one side over to the other and pinch the seams together, creating a seal. Fold corners over and do the same; repeat until all dough is used.
8. Place rolls on a large 9-by-13-inch baking sheet and bake at 350°F for about 25 mins or until slightly golden brown.
9. Remove rolls and allow to cool on a cooling rack for 10 to 15 minutes before eating; serve warm.

NUTRITIONAL INFO: CALORIES: 142, SODIUM: 329 MG, DIETARY Fiber: 1.1 g, Fat: 3.7 g, Carbs: 23.7 g, Protein: 3.7 g.

Wine and Cheese Bread

Wine and cheese come together in this recipe for one delicious loaf of bread. Serve alongside a bottle of your favorite wine with charcuterie and more cheese for one fun evening with friends.

SERVINGS: 12 | PREP TIME: 5 MINUTES | COOK TIME: 3 HOURS

INGREDIENTS:

- 3/4 cup white wine
- 1/2 cup white cheddar or gruyere cheese, shredded
- 1 1/2 tablespoons butter
- 1/2 teaspoon salt
- 3/4 teaspoon sugar
- 2 1/4 cups bread flour
- 1 1/2 teaspoons active dry yeast

DIRECTIONS:

1. Add liquid ingredients to the bread maker pan.
2. Add dry ingredients, except yeast, to the bread pan.
3. Use your fingers to form a well-like hole in the flour where you will pour the yeast; yeast must never come into contact with a liquid when you are adding the ingredients.
4. Carefully pour the yeast into the well.
5. Select Basic bread setting, light crust color, and press Start.
6. Allow to cool on a wire rack before serving.

NUTRITIONAL INFO: CALORIES: 132, SODIUM: 138 MG, DIETARY Fiber: 0.7 g, Fat: 3.3 g, Carbs: 18.8 g, Protein: 3.8 g.

Cheesy Sausage Loaf

Bake up something different for brunch or breakfast with this delicious recipe. Serve alongside scrambled eggs and fried apples, or a delicious spring salad, for an amazing meal.

SERVINGS: 12 | PREP TIME: 25 MINUTES | COOK TIME: 3 HOURS

INGREDIENTS:

- 1 cup warm water
- 4 teaspoons butter, softened
- 1 1/4 teaspoons salt
- 1 teaspoon sugar
- 3 cups bread flour
- 2 1/4 teaspoons active dry yeast
- 1 pound pork sausage roll, cooked and drained
- 1 1/2 cups Italian cheese, shredded
- 1/4 teaspoon garlic powder

- Pinch of black pepper
- 1 egg, lightly beaten
- Flour, for surface

DIRECTIONS:

1. Add the first five ingredients to the bread maker pan in order listed above.
2. Make a well in the flour; pour the yeast into the hole.
3. Select Dough cycle and press Start.
4. Turn kneaded dough onto a lightly floured surface and roll into a 16-by-10-inch rectangle. Cover with plastic wrap and let rest for 10 minutes
5. Combine sausage, cheese, garlic powder and pepper in a mixing bowl.
6. Spread sausage mixture evenly over the dough to within one 1/2 inch of edges. Start with a long side and roll up like a jelly roll, pinch seams to seal, and tuck ends under.
7. Place the loaf seam-side down on a greased baking sheet. Cover and let rise in a warm place for 30 minutes.
8. Preheat an oven to 350°F and bake 20 minutes.
9. Brush with egg and bake an additional 15 to 20 minutes until golden brown.
10. Remove to a cooling rack and serve warm.

NUTRITIONAL INFO: CALORIES: 172, SODIUM: 350 MG, DIETARY Fiber: 1.1 g, Fat: 4.7 g, Carbs: 27.1 g, Protein: 5.1 g.

Rosemary Focaccia Bread

A delicious, hearty loaf that is a tasty change from onion focaccia, this bread is great served on its own or as the base of any sandwich. Of course, you can also enjoy it with cheese and wine or your favorite soups and salads for a special treat.

SERVINGS: 4 - 6 | PREP TIME: 10 MINUTES | COOK TIME: 3 HOURS

INGREDIENTS:

- 1 cup, plus 3 tablespoons water
- 1 tablespoon extra-virgin olive oil
- 1 teaspoon salt
- 2 teaspoons fresh rosemary, chopped
- 3 cups bread flour
- 1 1/2 teaspoons instant yeast
- For the topping:
- 3 tablespoons olive oil

- Coarse salt
- Red pepper flakes

DIRECTIONS:

1. Add water, oil, salt, rosemary, and flour to the bread maker pan.
2. Make a well in the center of the dry ingredients and add the yeast.
3. Select Dough cycle and press Start.
4. Transfer finished dough to a floured surface.
5. Cover and let rest for 5 minutes.
6. Form dough into a smooth ball and roll into a 12-inch round.
7. Place on a 12-inch pizza pan that has been lightly greased with olive oil. Poke dough randomly with fingertips to form dimples. Brush top with olive oil and sprinkle with salt and red pepper flakes to taste.
8. Let rise uncovered in warm, draft-free space for about 30 minutes.
9. Bake at 425°F for 18 to 22 minutes or until done.
10. Serve warm.

NUTRITIONAL INFO: CALORIES: 312, SODIUM: 390 MG, DIETARY Fiber: 2.1 g, Fat: 10.1 g, Carbs: 48.3 g, Protein: 6.9 g.

Caramelized Onion Focaccia Bread

This delicious loaf makes the perfect base for any Italian-style sandwich. Try stuffing it with prosciutto or ham, and lettuce, tomatoes, olive oil and vinaigrette!

SERVINGS: 4 – 6 | PREP TIME: 15 MINUTES | COOK TIME: 3 HOURS

INGREDIENTS:

- 3/4 cup water
- 2 tablespoons olive oil
- 1 tablespoon sugar
- 1 teaspoon salt
- 2 cups flour
- 1 1/2 teaspoons yeast
- 3/4 cup mozzarella cheese, shredded
- 2 tablespoons parmesan cheese, shredded
- Onion topping:

- 3 tablespoons butter
- 2 medium onions
- 2 cloves garlic, minced

DIRECTIONS:

1. Place all ingredients, except cheese and onion topping, in your bread maker in the order listed above.
2. Grease a large baking sheet.
3. Pat dough into a 12-inch circle on the pan; cover and let rise in warm place for about 30 minutes.
4. Melt butter in large frying pan over medium-low heat. Cook onions and garlic in butter 15 minutes, stirring often, until onions are caramelized.
5. Preheat an oven to 400°F.
6. Make deep depressions across the dough at 1-inch intervals with the handle of a wooden spoon.
7. Spread the onion topping over dough and sprinkle with cheeses.
8. Bake 15 to 20 minutes or until golden brown. Cut into wedges and serve warm.

NUTRITIONAL INFO: CALORIES: 286, SODIUM: 482 MG, DIETARY Fiber: 2.2 g, Fat: 12 g, Carbs: 38.1 g, Protein: 6.8 g.

Cajun Bread

One spicy treat, you'll adore this delicious Cajun bread recipe. Serve it up with your favorite Cajun-inspired dishes, or alongside any meal for a special spice kick.

SERVINGS: 12 | PREP TIME: 5 MINUTES | COOK TIME: 2 HOURS 10 MINUTES

INGREDIENTS:

- 1/2 cup water
- 1/4 cup onion, chopped fine
- 1/4 cup green bell pepper, chopped fine
- 2 teaspoons garlic, chopped fine
- 2 teaspoons butter, softened
- 2 cups bread flour
- 1 tablespoon sugar
- 1 teaspoon Cajun seasoning
- 1 teaspoon active dry yeast

DIRECTIONS:

1. Measure all ingredients except yeast into bread maker in order listed above.
2. Make a well in the center of the dry ingredients and add the yeast.
3. Select Basic cycle, medium or dark crust color, and press Start; do not use delay cycle.
4. Remove from pan and cool on wire rack before serving.

NUTRITIONAL INFO: CALORIES: 89, SODIUM: 10 MG, DIETARY FIBER: 0.7 g, Fat: 0.9 g, Carbs: 17.6 g, Protein: 2.4 g.

Tomato Basil Bread

Slightly sweet aromatic bread is sure to turn your kitchen into something fantastic when you whip up this recipe. The taste of red pepper and sweet basil mixed with a hint of tomato produces one delicious loaf to serve just on its own.

SERVINGS: 16 | PREP TIME: 15 MINUTES | COOK TIME: 4 HOURS

INGREDIENTS:

- 3/4 cup warm water
- 1/4 cup fresh basil, minced
- 1/4 cup parmesan cheese, grated
- 3 tablespoons tomato paste
- 1 tablespoon sugar
- 1 tablespoon olive oil
- 1 teaspoon salt
- 1/4 teaspoon crushed red pepper flakes

- 2 1/2 cups bread flour
- 1 package active dry yeast
- Flour, for surface

DIRECTIONS:

1. Add ingredients, except yeast, to bread maker pan in above listed order.
2. Make a well in the flour; pour the yeast into the hole.
3. Select Dough cycle and press Start.
4. Turn finished dough out onto a floured surface and knead until smooth and elastic, about 3 to 5 minutes.
5. Place in a greased bowl, turning once to grease top. Cover and let rise in a warm place until doubled, about 1 hour.
6. Punch dough down and knead for 1 minute.
7. Shape into a round loaf. Place on a greased baking sheet. Cover and let rise until doubled, about 1 hour.
8. With a sharp knife, cut a large "X" in top of loaf. Bake at 375°F for 35-40 minutes or until golden brown.
9. Remove from pan and cool on a cooling rack before serving.

NUTRITIONAL INFO: CALORIES: 91, SODIUM: 172 MG, DIETARY FIBER: 0.8 g, Fat: 1.5 g, Carbs: 16.5 g, Protein: 2.8 g.

Pizza Dough

Pizza lovers will fall fast for this yummy homemade pizza dough! That's right, you can whip up delicious pizza dough anytime you please with this easy and tasty bread maker recipe.

SERVINGS: 12 - 14 | PREP TIME: 15 MINUTES | COOK TIME: 1 HOUR 30 MINUTES

INGREDIENTS:

- 1 1/4 cups water
- 3 cups bread flour
- 1 teaspoon milk powder
- 1 tablespoon sugar
- 1 teaspoon salt
- 1 tablespoon yeast

DIRECTIONS:

1. Add ingredients to the bread maker pan in the order listed above.
2. Select Dough cycle and press Start.
3. When finished, prepare dough by rolling it out in a pizza pan about to a 1-inch thickness.
4. Top with your favorite sauce, then cheese, then other toppings like pepperoni or veggies.
5. Bake at 425°F for 15 to 20 minutes or until crust is golden on the edges.
6. Enjoy hot!

NUTRITIONAL INFO: CALORIES: 103, SODIUM: 168 MG, DIETARY Fiber: 0.9 g, Fat: 0.3 g, Carbs: 21.7 g, Protein: 3.1 g.

Parsley and Chive Pull-Apart Rolls

These delicious savory rolls are a great accompaniment to almost any dish, but they go especially well with Italian-style recipes. You can even dip them in olive oil!

SERVINGS: 16 | PREP TIME: 20 MINUTES | COOKING TIME: 3 HOURS

INGREDIENTS:

- 1 cup buttermilk
- 6 tablespoons unsalted butter, cut into 6 pieces
- 3 2/3 cups all-purpose flour
- 2 1/4 teaspoons instant yeast
- 1/3 cup granulated sugar
- 1 teaspoon salt
- 3 large egg yolks
- 1/4 cup chives, chopped
- 1/4 cup parsley, chopped

- For the topping:
- 1/4 cup butter, melted

DIRECTIONS:

1. Combine the buttermilk and the 6 tablespoons butter in a small saucepan and warm until the butter melts, stirring continuously. Add the packet of instant yeast and allow to stand for five minutes.
2. Mix the egg yolks with a fork and add to the above mixture and blend.
3. Combine the flour, sugar, salt and herbs.
4. Add first the wet then the dry ingredients to your bread machine.
5. Set on Dough cycle and press Start.
6. Lightly grease a 9-by-13-inch glass baking dish.
7. Turn the dough out onto a clean work surface and press down gently. If the dough is too sticky add a little flour to the work surface. Using a bench scraper or a chef's knife, divide the dough into 16 equal pieces
8. Work one piece of dough at a time into a ball; keep the others covered with plastic wrap until ready to bake.
9. Cover the entire baking dish with plastic wrap and let the balls rise in a warm space, about 40 to 60 minutes.
10. Preheat an oven to 375°F and bake 20 to 25 minutes, or until lightly golden brown.
11. Remove from the oven and brush the tops with melted butter, serve warm.

NUTRITIONAL INFO: CALORIES: 196, SODIUM: 201 MG, DIETARY Fiber: 0.9 g, Fat: 8.4 g, Carbs: 26.5 g, Protein: 3.8 g.

Garlic Basil Knots

Garlic knots are so easy to bake right in the comfort of your own kitchen with the help of a bread machine! Just follow this easy recipe and you'll have warm garlic knots seasoned to perfection in no time.

SERVINGS: 10 | PREP TIME: 15 MINUTES | COOK TIME: 1 HOUR 45 MINUTES

INGREDIENTS:

- 1 cup water
- 2 tablespoons butter, softened
- 1 egg, room temperature
- 3 1/4 cups all-purpose flour
- 1/4 cup sugar
- 1 teaspoon salt
- 3 teaspoons regular active dry yeast
- For the topping:
- 2 tablespoons butter, melted

- 2 cloves garlic, minced
- 3 fresh basil leaves, chopped fine
- Flour, for surface

DIRECTIONS:

1. Add all dough ingredients in the bread machine in the order listed.
2. Select the Dough cycle and press Start.
3. Place parchment paper on a baking sheet and coat with cooking spray.
4. Flatten the dough onto a well-floured surface and cut into strips using a pizza cutter.
5. Tie each strip into a knot, making sure to keep them well-floured so they don't stick together. Place knots on the baking sheet and cover with a cloth; set in a warm place to rise for 30 minutes.
6. Preheat oven to 400°F and bake 9 to 12 minutes or until golden brown.
7. Serve warm!

NUTRITIONAL INFO: CALORIES: 218, SODIUM: 274 MG, DIETARY Fiber: 1.4 g, Fat: 5.5 g, Carbs: 36.7 g, Protein: 5.3 g.

FRUIT, VEGETABLE, HERBED & SPICED BREADS

Cranberry Walnut Wheat Bread

SERVINGS: 12 | PREP TIME: 15 MINUTES | COOK TIME: 3 HOURS 30 MINUTES

INGREDIENTS:

- 1 cup warm water
- 1 tablespoon molasses
- 2 tablespoons butter
- 1 teaspoon salt
- 2 cups 100% whole wheat flour
- 1 cup unbleached flour
- 2 tablespoons dry milk
- 1 cup cranberries
- 1 cup walnuts, chopped
- 2 teaspoons active dry yeast

DIRECTIONS:

1. Add the liquid ingredients to the bread maker pan.
2. Add the dry ingredients, except the yeast, walnuts and cranberries.
3. Make a well in the center of the bread flour and add the yeast.
4. Insert the pan into your bread maker and secure the lid.
5. Select Wheat Bread setting, choose your preferred crust color, and press Start.
6. Add cranberries and walnuts after first kneading cycle is finished.
7. Remove the bread from the oven and turn it out of the pan onto a cooling rack and allow it to cool completely before slicing.

NUTRITIONAL INFO: CALORIES: 126, SODIUM: 211 MG, DIETARY Fiber: 3.8 g, Fat: 2.6 g, Carbs: 23.2 g, Protein: 4.5 g.

Pineapple Carrot Bread

Sweet bread is delicious served next to savory soups! Enjoy this recipe, served with butter, alongside cream of tomato or red pepper bisque for a delicious meal.

SERVINGS: 12 | PREP TIME: 5 MINUTES | COOK TIME: 3 HOURS

INGREDIENTS:

- 1 (8-ounce) can crushed pineapple, with juice
- 1/2 cup carrots, shredded
- 2 eggs
- 2 tablespoons butter
- 4 cups bread flour
- 3 tablespoons sugar
- 1 teaspoon salt
- 3/4 teaspoon ground ginger
- 1 1/4 teaspoons active dry yeast

DIRECTIONS:

1. Add all of the ingredients (except yeast) to the bread maker pan in the order listed above.
2. Make a well in the center of the dry ingredients and add the yeast.
3. Select the Basic bread cycle and press Start.
4. Transfer baked loaf to a cooling rack for 15 minutes before slicing to serve.

NUTRITIONAL INFO: CALORIES: 203, SODIUM: 222 MG, DIETARY Fiber: 1.6 g, Fat: 3.1 g, Carbs: 38 g, Protein: 5.6 g.

Cinnamon Rolls

Cinnamon rolls are the perfect sweet treat for any breakfast or brunch. Serve on their own with a cup of tea or coffee, or enjoy with eggs, bacon, and fried potatoes for a decadent meal.

SERVINGS: 18 | PREP TIME: 25 MINUTES | COOK TIME: 3 HOURS

INGREDIENTS:

- 1 1/3 cups warm water
- 1 stick of butter, cut into small chunks
- 5 tablespoons sugar
- 1 egg
- 1 teaspoon salt
- 3 cups all-purpose flour
- 1 1/2 cups bread flour
- 1/4 cup powdered milk

- 1 tablespoon dry active yeast
- For the Filling:
- 1 cup sugar
- 1 1/2 tablespoons ground cinnamon
- 1/2 cup butter, softened
- For the Icing:
- 4 cups powdered sugar
- 2 tablespoons melted butter
- 1/2 teaspoon vanilla extract
- 4 tablespoons milk

DIRECTIONS:

1. Place the ingredients (except yeast) for the dough in your bread machine in the order listed.
2. Make a well in the center of the dry ingredients and add the yeast.
3. Select Dough cycle and press Start.
4. Split kneaded dough into two mounds.
5. On a lightly floured surface, roll one mound of your dough out into a rectangle.
6. Baste with half of the melted butter.
7. Sprinkle half of the cinnamon sugar over the melted butter making sure to cover as much surface with the filling as you can.
8. Starting at one of the short ends of your rectangle of dough, roll it up and brush the outside of roll with melted butter.
9. Slice the dough into about 1-inch pieces.
10. Place pinwheels on greased baking sheet next to one another.
11. Repeat the steps above with the second mound of dough.
12. Cover assembled dough with a light towel and let rise for 25-30 minutes.

13. Bake at 350°F for 17 minutes or until lightly brown on top.
14. Combine icing ingredients and cover rolls when removed from the oven; allow to cool 10 minutes before serving.

NUTRITIONAL INFO: CALORIES: 397, SODIUM: 214 MG, DIETARY Fiber: 0.9 g, Fat: 10.7 g, Carbs: 74.9 g, Protein: 3.8 g.

Brown Sugar Date Nut Swirl Bread

Brown sugar date nut swirl bread has just the right amount of sweet, so you can eat it on its own like a cake slice or muffin. It's delicious served warm with coffee or Earl Grey tea. For an exciting change, add peanut butter for an energizing snack!

SERVINGS: 16 | PREP TIME: 15 MINUTES | COOK TIME: 2 HOURS 30 MINUTES

INGREDIENTS:

- 1 cup milk
- 1 large egg
- 4 tablespoons butter
- 4 tablespoons sugar
- 1 teaspoon salt
- 4 cups flour
- 1 2/3 teaspoons yeast
- For the filling:

- 1/2 cup packed brown sugar
- 1 cup walnuts, chopped
- 1 cup medjool dates, pitted and chopped
- 2 teaspoons cinnamon
- 2 teaspoons clove spice
- 1 1/3 tablespoons butter
- Powdered sugar, sifted

DIRECTIONS:

1. Add wet ingredients to the bread maker pan.
2. Mix flour, sugar and salt and add to pan.
3. Make a well in the center of the dry ingredients and add the yeast.
4. Select the Dough cycle and press Start.
5. Punch the dough down and allow it to rest in a warm place.
6. Mix the brown sugar with walnuts, dates and spices; set aside.
7. Roll the dough into a rectangle, on a lightly floured surface.
8. Baste with a tablespoon of butter, add the filling.
9. Start from the short side and roll the dough to form a jelly roll shape.
10. Place the roll into a greased loaf pan and cover.
11. Let it rise in a warm place, until nearly doubled in size; about 30 minutes.
12. Bake at 350°F for approximately 30 minutes.
13. Cover with foil during the last 10 minutes of cooking.
14. Transfer to a cooling rack for 15 minutes; sprinkle with the powdered sugar and serve.

NUTRITIONAL INFO: CALORIES: 227, SODIUM: 197 MG, DIETARY Fiber: 1.5 g, Fat: 8.3 g, Carbs: 33.1 g, Protein: 5.5 g.

Cinnamon Pull-Apart Bread

Pull-apart bread doesn't have to be savory, and you can bake up sweet pull-apart treats in your bread maker just as easily! These delicately sweet pull-apart rolls will be a popular family treat, especially served with butter.

SERVINGS: 16 | PREP TIME: 15 MINUTES | COOK TIME: 3 HOURS

INGREDIENTS:

- 1/3 cup whole milk
- 4 tablespoons unsalted butter
- 1/4 cup warm water
- 1 teaspoon pure vanilla extract
- 2 large eggs
- 3 cups all-purpose flour
- 1/4 cup sugar

- 1/2 teaspoon salt
- 2 1/4 teaspoons active dry yeast
- For the Filling:
- 4 tablespoons unsalted butter, melted until browned (will smell like warm caramel)
- 1 cup sugar
- 2 teaspoons ground cinnamon
- Pinch of ground nutmeg

DIRECTIONS:

1. Add milk and butter to a saucepan and heat on medium-low until the butter melts; add liquid to the bread maker.
2. Add the rest of the ingredients (except yeast) in the order listed.
3. Make a well in the center of the dry ingredients and add the yeast.
4. Select Dough cycle and press Start.
5. When the dough is done, roll it out into a big sheet of dough, and brush the dough with the browned butter.
6. Combine sugar cinnamon and nutmeg in a mixing bowl and sprinkle over buttered dough.
7. Cut the dough into long thin strips and cut the strips into squares. Stack in threes, and place the dough squares next to one another in a greased bread pan.
8. Let rise in a warm place until doubled in size; cover with plastic wrap and refrigerate overnight to bake for breakfast.
9. Preheat an oven to 350°F.
10. Bake for 30 to 35 minutes, until the top is very golden brown.
11. When bread is done, transfer to a plate to cool and serve warm.

Nutritional Info: Calories: 210, Sodium: 126 mg, Dietary Fiber: 0.9 g, Fat: 6.8 g, Carbs: 34.3 g, Protein: 3.7 g.

Banana Split Loaf

Rich and decadent, this bread is perfect for dessert. Nutty, chocolatey and full of banana goodness, it's almost like eating a banana split. Try with a smear of Nutella spread for a truly sweet snack.

SERVINGS: 12 | PREP TIME: 10 MINUTES | COOK TIME: 1 HOUR

INGREDIENTS:

- 2 eggs
- 1/3 cup butter, melted
- 2 tablespoons whole milk
- 2 overripe bananas, mashed
- 2 cups all-purpose flour
- 2/3 cups sugar
- 1 1/4 teaspoons baking powder
- 1/2 teaspoon baking soda
- 1/2 teaspoon salt

- 1 cup chopped walnuts
- 1/2 cup chocolate chips

DIRECTIONS:

1. Pour eggs, butter, milk and bananas into the bread maker pan and set aside.
2. Stir together all dry ingredients in a large mixing bowl.
3. Add dry ingredients to bread maker pan.
4. Set to Basic setting, medium crust color, and press Start.
5. Remove bread and place on a cooling rack before serving.

NUTRITIONAL INFO: CALORIES: 260, SODIUM: 203 MG, DIETARY Fiber: 1.6 g, Fat: 11.3 g, Carbs: 35.9 g, Protein: 5.2 g.

Cranberry Orange Pecan Bread

Cool cranberries and bright oranges come together to give you one luscious loaf of dessert-style bread. You'll love serving this warm with butter or using it for the base of a French Toast recipe with a touch of cinnamon.

SERVINGS: 16 | PREP TIME: 5 MINUTES | COOK TIME: 2 HOURS 50 MINUTES

INGREDIENTS:

- 1 cup water
- 1/4 cup orange juice
- 2 teaspoons salt
- 1/3 cup sugar
- 2 1/2 tablespoons nonfat dry milk
- 2 1/2 tablespoons butter, cubed
- 4 cups bread flour
- 2 1/2 teaspoons orange zest

- 2 1/2 teaspoons bread machine yeast
- 1/2 cup dried cranberries
- 1/2 cup pecans, chopped

DIRECTIONS:

1. Set aside cranberries and pecans, then place all other ingredients in the bread maker pan in order listed.
2. Choose Sweet cycle, light crust and press Start.
3. Add cranberries and pecans at the end of the kneading cycle.
4. Transfer to a plate and let cool 10 minutes before slicing with a bread knife.

NUTRITIONAL INFO: CALORIES: 247 SODIUM: 311 DIETARY FIBER: 2.6 g, Fat: 11.5 g, Carbs: 31.5 g, Protein: 5.4 g.

Raisin Bread

Bread sweetened with sun-kissed raisins can be delicious for breakfast, brunch or afternoon snack. Serve this sweet treat with your favorite cup of hot tea, coffee or cocoa and enjoy with friends! It's also delicious spread with butter and jam.

SERVINGS: 12 | PREP TIME: 5 MINUTES | COOK TIME: 3 HOURS

INGREDIENTS:

- 1 cup warm water
- 3 tablespoons vegetable oil
- 3 cups flour
- 1 teaspoon cinnamon
- 1/8 teaspoon nutmeg
- 1/3 cup sugar
- 1 1/2 teaspoons salt
- 1 packet instant dry yeast

- 3/4 cup raisins

DIRECTIONS:

1. Add the water and oil to the bread maker.
2. Add flour and sprinkle with cinnamon and nutmeg.
3. On top of the flour, add sugar to one corner of the bread maker, salt in the other corner and yeast in another corner, so the yeast is not touching sugar and salt.
4. Set to Basic bread cycle, medium crust color, and press Start.
5. Add the raisins when the dough cycle is finished.
6. When the baking cycle is finished, transfer to a cooling rack for 15 minutes before slicing.

NUTRITIONAL INFO: CALORIES: 193, SODIUM: 1068 MG, DIETARY Fiber: 1.3 g, Fat: 3.8 g, Carbs: 36.8 g, Protein: 3.5 g.

Banana Bread

Looking to a bake a really sweet treat? Try this scrumptious banana bread recipe that will have your whole family craving more, even when the loaf is gobbled up!

SERVINGS: 12 | PREP TIME: 10 MINUTES | COOK TIME: 2 HOURS 40 MINUTES

INGREDIENTS:

- 3 large, overripe bananas
- 8 tablespoons sugar
- 2 eggs
- 2 cups flour, sifted
- 1 teaspoon salt
- 1 teaspoon baking powder
- 1/2 teaspoon vanilla extract
- 1 teaspoon cinnamon
- 2 tablespoons walnuts, chopped

- Butter, for greasing pan

DIRECTIONS:

1. Mash the bananas with a fork and add the sugar in a large mixing bowl until smooth.
2. Butter the bread maker loaf pan; pour in the banana mixture.
3. Add the eggs, flour, and remaining dry ingredients.
4. Select Sweet cycle setting, medium crust color, and press Start.
5. Transfer to a cooling rack for 15 minutes before slicing to serve.

NUTRITIONAL INFO: CALORIES: 156, SODIUM: 205 MG, DIETARY Fiber: 1.6 g, Fat: 1.8 g, Carbs: 32.2 g, Protein: 3.8 g.

Zucchini Bread

Sweet and delicate, this loaf is the perfect way to enjoy a serving of veggies and a delicious treat. Serve it warm right out of the oven or chilled in the refrigerator - either way, it's fabulous.

SERVINGS: 12 | PREP TIME: 15 MINUTES | COOK TIME: 3 HOURS 40 MINUTES

INGREDIENTS:

- 1/2 teaspoon salt
- 1 cup sugar
- 1 tablespoon pumpkin pie spice
- 1 tablespoon baking powder
- 1 teaspoon pure vanilla extract
- 1/3 cup milk
- 1/2 cup vegetable oil
- 2 eggs
- 2 cups bread flour

- 1 1/2 teaspoons active dry yeast or bread machine yeast
- 1 cup shredded zucchini, raw and unpeeled
- 1 cup of chopped walnuts (optional)

DIRECTIONS:

1. Add all of the ingredients for the zucchini bread into the bread maker pan in the order listed above, reserving yeast.
2. Make a well in the center of the dry ingredients and add the yeast.
3. Select Wheat bread cycle, medium crust color, and press Start.
4. Transfer to a cooling rack for 10 to 15 minutes before slicing to serve.

NUTRITIONAL INFO: CALORIES: 304, SODIUM: 114 MG, DIETARY Fiber: 1.6 g, Fat: 16.4 g, Carbs: 35.5 g, Protein: 6.1 g.

Pumpkin Coconut Almond Bread

What do you get when you combine hearty pumpkin, sweet coconut, and delicious almonds? One amazing loaf of bread! Be sure to serve warm with your favorite hot drinks for one decadent snack or coffee break.

SERVINGS: 12 | PREP TIME: 5 MINUTES | COOK TIME: 3 HOURS

INGREDIENTS:

- 1/3 cup vegetable oil
- 3 large eggs
- 1 1/2 cups canned pumpkin puree
- 1 cup sugar
- 1 1/2 teaspoons baking powder
- 1/2 teaspoon baking soda
- 1/4 teaspoon salt
- 1 tablespoon allspice

- 3 cups all-purpose flour
- 1/2 cup coconut flakes, plus a small handful for the topping
- 2/3 cup slivered almonds, plus a tablespoonful for the topping
- Non-stick cooking spray

DIRECTIONS:

1. Spray bread maker pan with non-stick cooking spray.
2. Mix oil, eggs, and pumpkin in a large mixing bowl.
3. Mix remaining ingredients together in a separate mixing bowl.
4. Add wet ingredients to bread maker pan, and dry ingredients on top.
5. Select Dough cycle and press Start.
6. Open lid and sprinkle top of bread with reserved coconut and almonds.
7. Set to Rapid for 1 hour 30 minutes and bake.
8. Cool for 10 minutes on a wire rack before serving.

NUTRITIONAL INFO: CALORIES: 302, SODIUM: 124 MG, DIETARY Fiber: 2.8 g, Fat: 11.5 g, Carbs: 45.4 g, Protein: 6.4 g.

Cinnamon Raisin Breadsticks

Looking for a sweet treat that the kids can help make? These delicious breadsticks are a great after-school snack or rainy day activity that kids will love.

SERVINGS: 16 | PREP TIME: 15 MINUTES | COOK TIME: 3 HOURS

INGREDIENTS:

- 1 cup milk
- 2 tablespoons water
- 1 tablespoon oil
- 3/4 teaspoon salt
- 2 tablespoons brown sugar
- 3 cups bread flour
- 1 teaspoon cinnamon
- 1 tablespoon active dry yeast
- 1/2 cup raisins

- Vanilla icing, for glaze

DIRECTIONS:

1. Preheat oven to 475°F.
2. Mix the cinnamon into the bread flour.
3. Add milk, water, oil, salt and brown sugar to the bread maker pan, then add the flour/cinnamon mixture.
4. Make a well in the center of the dry ingredients and add the yeast.
5. Set on Dough cycle and press Start.
6. Take out the dough out and punch down; let rest for 10 minutes.
7. Roll dough into a 12-by-8-inch rectangle.
8. Sprinkle raisins on one half of the dough and gently press them into the dough.
9. Fold the dough in half and gently roll and stretch dough back out into a rectangle.
10. Cut into strips, then twist.
11. Line a baking sheet with parchment paper and bake for 4 minutes.
12. Place on 2 baking sheets that have been lined with parchment paper. Reduce oven temperature to 350°F.
13. Brush breadsticks lightly with water and return to oven and bake 20-25 minutes.
14. Cool on a wire rack.
15. Glaze with vanilla icing and serve.

NUTRITIONAL INFO: CALORIES: 121, SODIUM: 117 MG, DIETARY Fiber: 1 g, Fat: 1.4 g, Carbs: 23.7 g, Protein: 3.4 g.

Monkey Bread

Nothing says brunch like a decadent monkey bread covered in oodles of cinnamon and sweet sugar glaze. That's why this is one of my favorite recipes for the Bread Maker!

SERVINGS: 12 - 15 | PREP TIME: 25 MINUTES | COOK TIME: 2 HOURS

INGREDIENTS:

- 1 cup water
- 1 cup butter, unsalted
- 2 tablespoons butter, softened
- 3 cups all-purpose flour
- 1 teaspoon ground cinnamon
- 1 teaspoon salt
- 1/4 cup white sugar
- 2 1/2 teaspoons active dry yeast
- 1 cup brown sugar, packed

- 1 cup raisins
- Flour, for surface

DIRECTIONS:

1. Add ingredients, except 1 cup butter, brown sugar, raisins and yeast, to bread maker pan in order listed above.
2. Make a well in the center of the dry ingredients and add the yeast. Make sure that no liquid comes in contact with the yeast.
3. Select Dough cycle and press Start.
4. Place finished dough on floured surface and knead 10 times.
5. Melt one cup of butter in small saucepan.
6. Stir in brown sugar and raisins and mix until smooth. Remove from heat.
7. Cut dough into one inch chunks.
8. Drop one chunk at a time into the butter sugar mixture. Thoroughly coat dough pieces, then layer them loosely in a greased Bundt pan.
9. Let rise in a warm, draft-free space; about 15 to 20 minutes.
10. Bake at 375°F for 20 to 25 minutes or until golden brown.
11. Remove from oven, plate, and serve warm.

NUTRITIONAL INFO: CALORIES: 294, SODIUM: 265. MG, DIETARY Fiber: 1.3 g, Fat: 14.1 g, Carbs: 40 g, Protein: 3.3 g.

GLUTEN-FREE BREADS

Gluten-Free Simple Sandwich Bread

Gluten free doesn't mean giving up your favorite foods, you just have to get creative. That's why this recipe is perfect for those that have gluten allergies or sensitivity!

SERVINGS: 12 | PREP TIME: 5 MINUTES | COOK TIME: 1 HOUR

INGREDIENTS:

- 1 1/2 cups sorghum flour
- 1 cup tapioca starch or potato starch (not potato flour!)
- 1/2 cup gluten-free millet flour or gluten-free oat flour
- 2 teaspoons xanthan gum
- 1 1/4 teaspoons fine sea salt
- 2 1/2 teaspoons gluten-free yeast for bread machines
- 1 1/4 cups warm water
- 3 tablespoons extra virgin olive oil
- 1 tablespoon honey or raw agave nectar

- 1/2 teaspoon mild rice vinegar or lemon juice
- 2 organic free-range eggs, beaten

DIRECTIONS:

1. Whisk together the dry ingredients except the yeast and set aside.
2. Add the liquid ingredients to the bread maker pan first, then gently pour the mixed dry ingredients on top of the liquid.
3. Make a well in the center of the dry ingredients and add the yeast.
4. Set for Rapid 1 hour 20 minutes, medium crust color, and press Start.
5. Transfer to a cooling rack for 15 minutes before slicing to serve.

NUTRITIONAL INFO: CALORIES: 137, SODIUM: 85 MG, DIETARY FIBER: 2.7 g, Fat: 4.6 g, Carbs: 22.1 g, Protein: 2.4 g.

Grain-Free Chia Bread

When you go grain free, you might think you have to cut some of your favorite foods out. This recipe will help you add them right back into your healthy diet!

SERVINGS: 12 | PREP TIME: 5 MINUTES | COOK TIME: 3 HOURS

INGREDIENTS:

- 1 cup warm water
- 3 large organic eggs, room temperature
- 1/4 cup olive oil
- 1 tablespoon apple cider vinegar
- 1 cup gluten-free chia seeds, ground to flour
- 1 cup almond meal flour
- 1/2 cup potato starch
- 1/4 cup coconut flour
- 3/4 cup millet flour

- 1 tablespoon xanthan gum
- 1 1/2 teaspoons salt
- 2 tablespoons sugar
- 3 tablespoons nonfat dry milk
- 6 teaspoons instant yeast

DIRECTIONS:

1. Whisk wet ingredients together and add to the bread maker pan.
2. Whisk dry ingredients, except yeast, together and add on top of wet ingredients.
3. Make a well in the dry ingredients and add yeast.
4. Select Whole Wheat cycle, light crust color, and press Start.
5. Allow to cool completely before serving.

NUTRITIONAL INFO: CALORIES: 375, SODIUM: 462 MG, DIETARY Fiber: 22.3 g, Fat: 18.3 g, Carbs: 42 g, Protein: 12.2 g.

Gluten-Free Brown Bread

A delicious brown bread alternative, this recipe is just as easy as any other bread maker bread recipe. You'll have fresh brown bread to serve as toast with butter,, or as the star of your favorite sandwiches!

SERVINGS: 12 | PREP TIME: 5 MINUTES | COOK TIME: 3 HOURS

NOTE

Because this recipe calls for extra water, the bake time is extra long.

INGREDIENTS:

- 2 large eggs, lightly beaten
- 1 3/4 cups warm water
- 3 tablespoons canola oil
- 1 cup brown rice flour

- 3/4 cup oat flour
- 1/4 cup tapioca starch
- 1 1/4 cups potato starch
- 1 1/2 teaspoons salt
- 2 tablespoons brown sugar
- 2 tablespoons gluten-free flaxseed meal
- 1/2 cup nonfat dry milk powder
- 2 1/2 teaspoons xanthan gum
- 3 tablespoons psyllium, whole husks
- 2 1/2 teaspoons gluten-free yeast for bread machines

DIRECTIONS:

1. Add the eggs, water and canola oil to the bread maker pan and stir until combined.
2. Whisk all of the dry ingredients except the yeast together in a large mixing bowl.
3. Add the dry ingredients on top of the wet ingredients.
4. Make a well in the center of the dry ingredients and add the yeast.
5. Set Gluten-Free cycle, medium crust color, and press Start.
6. When the bread is done, lay the pan on its side to cool before slicing to serve.

NUTRITIONAL INFO: CALORIES: 201, SODIUM: 390 MG, DIETARY Fiber: 10.6 g, Fat: 5.7 g, Carbs: 35.5 g, Protein: 5.1 g.

Easy Gluten-Free, Dairy-Free Bread

Even withliving a gluten-free and dairy-free lifestyle, you can still eat bread. Just use this delicious, easy recipe to bake up some fresh bread right in the comfort of your kitchen.

SERVINGS: 12 | PREP TIME: 15 MINUTES | COOK TIME: 2 HOURS 10 MINUTES

INGREDIENTS:

- 1 1/2 cups warm water
- 2 teaspoons active dry yeast
- 2 teaspoons sugar
- 2 eggs, room temperature
- 1 egg white, room temperature
- 1 1/2 tablespoons apple cider vinegar
- 4 1/2 tablespoons olive oil
- 3 1/3 cups multi-purpose gluten-free flour

DIRECTIONS:

1. Add the yeast and sugar to the warm water and stir to mix in a large mixing bowl; set aside until foamy, about 8 to 10 minutes.
2. Whisk the 2 eggs and 1 egg white together in a separate mixing bowl and add to baking pan of bread maker.
3. Add apple cider vinegar and oil to baking pan.
4. Add foamy yeast/water mixture to baking pan.
5. Add the multi-purpose gluten-free flour on top.
6. Set for Gluten-Free bread setting and Start.
7. Remove and invert pan onto a cooling rack to remove the bread from the baking pan. Allow to cool completely before slicing to serve.

NUTRITIONAL INFO: CALORIES: 241, SODIUM: 164 MG, DIETARY Fiber: 5.6 g, Fat: 6.8 g, Carbs: 41 g, Protein: 4.5 g.

Gluten-Free Sourdough Bread

Sourdough bread is delicious and rustic and tastes good with any soup or salads you love. No one will ever know this yummy loaf of crusty bread is also gluten free!

SERVINGS: 12 | PREP TIME: 5 MINUTES | COOK TIME: 3 HOURS

INGREDIENTS:

- 1 cup water
- 3 eggs
- 3/4 cup ricotta cheese
- 1/4 cup honey
- 1/4 cup vegetable oil
- 1 teaspoon cider vinegar
- 3/4 cup gluten-free sourdough starter
- 2 cups white rice flour
- 2/3 cup potato starch

- 1/3 cup tapioca flour
- 1/2 cup dry milk powder
- 3 1/2 teaspoons xanthan gum
- 1 1/2 teaspoons salt

DIRECTIONS:

1. Combine wet ingredients and pour into bread maker pan.
2. Mix together dry ingredients in a large mixing bowl, and add on top of the wet ingredients.
3. Select Gluten-Free cycle and press Start.
4. Remove the pan from the machine and allow the bread to remain in the pan for approximately 10 minutes.
5. Transfer to a cooling rack before slicing.

NUTRITIONAL INFO: CALORIES: 299, SODIUM: 327 MG, DIETARY Fiber: 1.0 g, Fat: 7.3 g, Carbs: 46 g, Protein: 5.2 g.

Gluten-Free Crusty Boule Bread

Crusty boules are delicious enjoyed as bread bowls when hollowed out and filled with your favorite soup. They're also great for entertaining guests with dips before a lovely dinner.

SERVINGS: 12 | PREP TIME: 15 MINUTES | COOK TIME: 3 HOURS

INGREDIENTS:

- 3 1/4 cups gluten-free flour mix
- 1 tablespoon active dry yeast
- 1 1/2 teaspoons kosher salt
- 1 tablespoon guar gum
- 1 1/3 cups warm water
- 2 large eggs, room temperature
- 2 tablespoons, plus 2 teaspoons olive oil
- 1 tablespoon honey

DIRECTIONS:

1. Combine all of the dry ingredients, except the yeast, in a large mixing bowl; set aside.
2. Whisk together the water, eggs, oil, and honey in a separate mixing bowl.
3. Pour the wet ingredients into the bread maker.
4. Add the dry ingredients on top of the wet ingredients.
5. Make a well in the center of the dry ingredients and add the yeast.
6. Set to Gluten-Free setting and press Start.
7. Remove baked bread and allow to cool completely. Hollow out and fill with soup or dip to use as a boule, or slice for serving.

NUTRITIONAL INFO: CALORIES: 480, SODIUM: 490 MG, DIETARY Fiber: 67.9 g, Fat: 3.2 g, Carbs: 103.9 g, Protein: 2.4 g.

Gluten-Free Potato Bread

Bake densely delicious potato bread at home that is 100% gluten free. This recipe is a great way to use leftover potatoes and really add luxurious-tasting bread to your gluten-free life!

SERVINGS: 12 | PREP TIME: 5 MINUTES | COOK TIME: 3 HOURS

INGREDIENTS:

- 1 medium russet potato, baked, or mashed leftovers
- 2 packets gluten-free quick yeast
- 3 tablespoons honey
- 3/4 cup warm almond milk
- 2 eggs, 1 egg white
- 3 2/3 cups almond flour
- 3/4 cup tapioca flour
- 1 teaspoon sea salt
- 1 teaspoon dried chives

- 1 tablespoon apple cider vinegar
- 1/4 cup olive oil

DIRECTIONS:

1. Combine all of the dry ingredients, except the yeast, in a large mixing bowl; set aside.
2. Whisk together the milk, eggs, oil, apple cider, and honey in a separate mixing bowl.
3. Pour the wet ingredients into the bread maker.
4. Add the dry ingredients on top of the wet ingredients.
5. Create a well in the dry ingredients and add the yeast.
6. Set to Gluten-Free bread setting, light crust color, and press Start.
7. Allow to cool completely before slicing.

NUTRITIONAL INFO: CALORIES: 232, SODIUM: 173 MG, DIETARY Fiber: 6.3 g, Fat: 13.2 g, Carbs: 17.4 g, Protein: 10.4 g.

Sorghum Bread Recipe

Soft bread is right at your gluten-free, healthy lifestyle fingertips when you bake up a loaf using this recipe. This tall loaf is great for sandwiches and making croutons!

SERVINGS: 12 | PREP TIME: 5 MINUTES | COOK TIME: 3 HOURS

INGREDIENTS:

- 1 1/2 cups sorghum flour
- 1 cup tapioca starch
- 1/2 cup brown or white sweet rice flour
- 1 teaspoon xanthan gum
- 1 teaspoon guar gum
- 1/2 teaspoon salt
- 3 tablespoons sugar
- 2 1/4 teaspoons instant yeast
- 3 eggs (room temperature, lightly beaten)

- 1/4 cup oil
- 1 1/2 teaspoons vinegar
- 3/4-1 cup milk (105 - 115°F)

DIRECTIONS:

1. Combine the dry ingredients in a mixing bowl, except for yeast.
2. Add the wet ingredients to the bread maker pan, then add the dry ingredients on top.
3. Make a well in the center of the dry ingredients and add the yeast.
4. Set to Basic bread cycle, light crust color, and press Start.
5. Remove and lay on its side to cool on a wire rack before serving.

NUTRITIONAL INFO: CALORIES: 169, SODIUM: 151 MG, DIETARY Fiber: 2.5 g, Fat: 6.3 g, Carbs: 25.8 g, Protein: 3.3 g.

Paleo Bread

Living a Paleo lifestyle doesn't mean giving up the things you love! You can still enjoy delicious bread made with paleo-friendly almond flour when you bake up this delicious recipe.

SERVINGS: 16 | PREP TIME: 10 MINUTES | COOK TIME: 3 HOURS 15 MINUTES

INGREDIENTS:

- 4 tablespoons chia seeds
- 1 tablespoon flax meal
- 3/4 cup, plus 1 tablespoon water
- 1/4 cup coconut oil
- 3 eggs, room temperature
- 1/2 cup almond milk
- 1 tablespoon honey
- 2 cups almond flour
- 1 1/4 cups tapioca flour

- 1/3 cup coconut flour
- 1 teaspoon salt
- 1/4 cup flax meal
- 2 teaspoons cream of tartar
- 1 teaspoon baking soda
- 2 teaspoons active dry yeast

DIRECTIONS:

1. Combine the chia seeds and tablespoon of flax meal in a mixing bowl; stir in the water and set aside.
2. Melt the coconut oil in a microwave-safe dish, and let it cool down to lukewarm.
3. Whisk in the eggs, almond milk and honey.
4. Whisk in the chia seeds and flax meal gel and pour it into the bread maker pan.
5. Stir the almond flour, tapioca flour, coconut flour, salt and 1/4 cup of flax meal together.
6. Mix the cream of tartar and baking soda in a separate bowl and combine it with the other dry ingredients.
7. Pour the dry ingredients into the bread machine.
8. Make a little well on top and add the yeast.
9. Start the machine on the Wheat cycle, light or medium crust color, and press Start.
10. Remove to cool completely before slicing to serve.

NUTRITIONAL INFO: CALORIES: 190, SODIUM: 243 MG, DIETARY Fiber: 5.2 g, Fat: 10.3 g, Carbs: 20.4 g, Protein: 4.5 g.

Gluten-Free Oat & Honey Bread

Oat and honey bread is a great way to add healthy carbohydrates to your gluten-free lifestyle. This bread is great for sandwiches, served as toast, and even great on its own just out of the oven.

SERVINGS: 12 | PREP TIME: 5 MINUTES | COOK TIME: 3 HOURS

INGREDIENTS:

- 1 1/4 cups warm water
- 3 tablespoons honey
- 2 eggs
- 3 tablespoons butter, melted
- 1 1/4 cups gluten-free oats
- 1 1/4 cups brown rice flour
- 1/2 cup potato starch
- 2 teaspoons xanthan gum
- 1 1/2 teaspoons sugar

- 3/4 teaspoon salt
- 1 1/2 tablespoons active dry yeast

DIRECTIONS:

1. Add ingredients in the order listed above, except for yeast.
2. Make a well in the center of the dry ingredients and add the yeast.
3. Select Gluten-Free cycle, light crust color, and press Start.
4. Remove bread and allow the bread to cool on its side on a cooling rack for 20 minutes before slicing to serve.

NUTRITIONAL INFO: CALORIES: 151, SODIUM: 265 MG, DIETARY Fiber: 4.3 g, Fat: 4.5 g, Carbs: 27.2 g, Protein: 3.5 g.

Gluten-Free Cinnamon Raisin Bread

Fruit bread is a great way to start the day! This recipe is best served warm or toasted with just a pat of butter or some honey.

SERVINGS: 12 | PREP TIME: 5 MINUTES | COOK TIME: 3 HOURS

INGREDIENTS:

- 3/4 cup almond milk
- 2 tablespoons flax meal
- 6 tablespoons warm water
- 1 1/2 teaspoons apple cider vinegar
- 2 tablespoons butter
- 1 1/2 tablespoons honey
- 1 2/3 cups brown rice flour
- 1/4 cup corn starch
- 2 tablespoons potato starch
- 1 1/2 teaspoons xanthan gum

- 1 tablespoon cinnamon
- 1/2 teaspoon salt
- 1 teaspoon active dry yeast
- 1/2 cup raisins

DIRECTIONS:

1. Mix together flax and water and let stand for 5 minutes.
2. Combine dry ingredients in a separate bowl, except for yeast.
3. Add wet ingredients to the bread machine.
4. Add the dry mixture on top and make a well in the middle of the dry mixture.
5. Add the yeast to the well.
6. Set to Gluten Free, light crust color, and press Start.
7. After first kneading and rise cycle, add raisins.
8. Remove to a cooling rack when baked and let cool for 15 minutes before slicing.

NUTRITIONAL INFO: CALORIES: 192, SODIUM: 173 MG, DIETARY Fiber: 4.4 g, Fat: 4.7 g, Carbs: 38.2 g, Protein: 2.7 g.

Gluten-Free Pumpkin Pie Bread

Perfect for fall to winter months, when the sky is grey and you feel like curling up with a cup of hot tea. You'll be digging out your favorite ugly sweater in no time...

SERVINGS: 12 | PREP TIME: 5 MINUTES | COOK TIME: 2 HOURS 50 MINUTES

INGREDIENTS:

- 1/4 cup olive oil
- 2 large eggs, beaten
- 1 tablespoon bourbon vanilla extract
- 1 cup canned pumpkin
- 4 tablespoons honey
- 1/4 teaspoon lemon juice
- 1/2 cup buckwheat flour
- 1/4 cup millet flour
- 1/4 cup sorghum flour

- 1/2 cup tapioca starch
- 1 cup light brown sugar
- 2 teaspoons baking powder
- 1 teaspoon baking soda
- 1/2 teaspoon sea salt
- 1 teaspoon xanthan gum
- 1 teaspoon ground cinnamon
- 1 teaspoon allspice
- 1-2 tablespoons peach juice

DIRECTIONS:

1. Mix dry ingredients together in a bowl and put aside.
2. Add wet ingredients to pan, except peach juice.
3. Add mixed dry ingredients to bread maker pan.
4. Set to Sweet bread cycle, light or medium crust color, and press Start.
5. As it begins to mix the ingredients, use a soft silicone spatula to scrape down the sides.
6. If the batter is stiff, add one tablespoon at a time of peach juice until the batter becomes slightly thinner than muffin batter.
7. Close the lid and allow to bake. Remove to a cooling rack for 20 minutes before slicing.

NUTRITIONAL INFO: CALORIES: 180, SODIUM: 229 MG, DIETARY Fiber: 2.5 g, Fat: 5.5 g, Carbs: 33.1 g, Protein: 2.4 g.

Gluten-Free Pizza Crust

Pizza lovers rejoice! Even though you are gluten free, with this recipe you can still have scrumptious, gooey pizza right in the comfort of your own home.

SERVINGS: 6 - 8 | PREP TIME: 10 MINUTES | COOK TIME: 2 HOURS

INGREDIENTS:

- 3 large eggs, room temperature
- 1/2 cup olive oil
- 1 cup milk
- 1/2 cup water
- 2 cups rice flour
- 1 cup cornstarch, and extra for dusting
- 1/2 cup potato starch
- 1/2 cup sugar
- 2 tablespoons yeast

- 3 teaspoons xanthan gum
- 1 teaspoon salt

DIRECTIONS:

1. Combine the wet ingredients in a separate bowl and pour into the bread maker pan.
2. Combine the dry ingredients except yeast and add to pan.
3. Make a well in the center of the dry ingredients and add the yeast.
4. Select Dough cycle and press Start.
5. When dough is finished, press it out on a surface lightly sprinkled with corn starch and create a pizza shape. Use this dough with your favorite toppings and pizza recipe!

NUTRITIONAL INFO: CALORIES: 463, SODIUM: 547 MG, DIETARY Fiber: 8.1 g, Fat: 15.8 g, Carbs: 79.2 g, Protein: 7.4 g.

Gluten-Free Whole Grain Bread

Whole grain bread doesn't have to be filled with wheat flour. You can whip up delicious gluten-free whole grain and still enjoy delicious, healthy bread!

SERVINGS: 12 | PREP TIME: 15 MINUTES | COOK TIME: 3 HOURS 40 MINUTES

INGREDIENTS:

- 2/3 cup sorghum flour
- 1/2 cup buckwheat flour
- 1/2 cup millet flour
- 3/4 cup potato starch
- 2 1/4 teaspoons xanthan gum
- 1 1/4 teaspoons salt
- 3/4 cup skim milk
- 1/2 cup water
- 1 tablespoon instant yeast

- 5 teaspoons agave nectar, separated
- 1 large egg, lightly beaten
- 4 tablespoons extra virgin olive oil
- 1/2 teaspoon cider vinegar
- 1 tablespoon poppy seeds

DIRECTIONS:

1. Whisk sorghum, buckwheat, millet, potato starch, xanthan gum, and sea salt in a bowl and set aside.
2. Combine milk and water in a glass measuring cup. Heat to between 110°F and 120°F; add 2 teaspoons of agave nectar and yeast and stir to combine. Cover and set aside for a few minutes.
3. Combine the egg, olive oil, remaining agave, and vinegar in another mixing bowl; add yeast and milk mixture. Pour wet ingredients into the bottom of your bread maker.
4. Top with dry ingredients.
5. Select Gluten-Free cycle, light color crust, and press Start.
6. After second kneading cycle sprinkle with poppy seeds.
7. Remove pan from bread machine. Leave the loaf in the pan for about 5 minutes before cooling on a rack.
8. Enjoy!

NUTRITIONAL INFO: CALORIES: 153, SODIUM: 346 MG, DIETARY Fiber: 4.1 g, Fat: 5.9 g, Carbs: 24.5 g, Protein: 3.3 g.

Gluten-Free Pull-Apart Rolls

This recipe mimics an all-American favorite: pull-apart rolls. How do you make gluten-free rolls that can pull apart? Try this and have some fun with it.

SERVINGS: 9 | PREP TIME: 5 MINUTES | COOK TIME: 2 HOURS

INGREDIENTS:

- 1 cup warm water
- 2 tablespoons butter, unsalted
- 1 egg, room temperature
- 1 teaspoon apple cider vinegar
- 2 3/4 cups gluten-free almond-blend flour
- 1 1/2 teaspoons xanthan gum
- 1/4 cup sugar
- 1 teaspoon salt
- 2 teaspoons active dry yeast

DIRECTIONS:

1. Add wet ingredients to the bread maker pan.
2. Mix dry ingredients except for yeast, and put in pan.
3. Make a well in the center of the dry ingredients and add the yeast.
4. Select Dough cycle and press Start.
5. Spray an 8-inch round cake pan with non-stick cooking spray.
6. When Dough cycle is complete, roll dough out into 9 balls, place in cake pan, and baste each with warm water.
7. Cover with a towel and let rise in a warm place for 1 hour.
8. Preheat oven to 400°F.
9. Bake for 26 to 28 minutes; until golden brown.
10. Brush with butter and serve.

NUTRITIONAL INFO: CALORIES: 568, SODIUM: 380 MG, DIETARY Fiber: 5.5 g, Fat: 10.5 g, Carbs: 116.3 g, Protein: 8.6 g.

INTERNATIONAL BREADS

Italian Panettone

Italian Christmas cake is a great way to get family and friends to gather at your house during the holidays. Try it toasted with a smear of butter.

SERVINGS: 16 | PREP TIME: 15 MINUTES | COOK TIME: 3 HOURS

INGREDIENTS:

- 3/4 cup warm water
- 4 large egg yolks
- 2 teaspoons vanilla extract
- 1/2 cup sugar
- 1 teaspoon lemon zest
- 1 teaspoon orange zest
- 1/2 teaspoon salt
- 1/2 cup unsalted butter, softened and cut into pieces

- 3 1/4 cups unbleached flour
- 1 package bread machine yeast
- 1/2 cup golden raisins
- 1/2 cup raisins
- 1 egg white, slightly beaten
- 4 sugar cubes, crushed

DIRECTIONS:

1. Add the water, egg yolks, vanilla, and zest to the bread maker pan.
2. Add the sugar, salt, and flour.
3. Lay pieces of butter around the outside of the pan on top of the flour.
4. Press a well into the flour and add the yeast.
5. Start the Dough cycle; at the second kneading cycle add golden raisins and raisins.
6. Let dough rise until doubled.
7. Prepare the pan/baking case: cut a circle of parchment paper to line the bottom of the 6-inch cake pan and spray with non-stick cooking spray.
8. Cut another piece of parchment to line the inside of the brown paper bag after you have cut the bottom out of the bag.
9. Fold the top edge down to form a cuff then spray the inside of the parchment with cooking spray. Place the paper case in the pan.
10. Punch the dough down and knead into a ball.
11. Add it to the paper-lined pan case and allow to rise until almost doubled.
12. Preheat the oven to 350°F.
13. Baste the top of the panettone dough with the beaten egg white and sprinkle with the crushed sugar cubes.

14. Bake for 30 minutes, then reduce heat to 325°F and bake another 30 minutes.

15. Remove from oven and allow to cool in pan for about 15 minutes, then cool on a rack until ready to serve.

NUTRITIONAL INFO: CALORIES: 201, SODIUM: 120 MG, DIETARY Fiber: 1 g, Fat: 7.2 g, Carbs: 30.6 g, Protein: 3.9 g

Bread of the Dead (Pan de Muertos)

A traditional cake served on All Souls Day, Bread of the Dead is delicious and should be consumed in memory of your loved ones.

SERVINGS: 12 | PREP TIME: 5 MINUTES | COOK TIME: 2 HOURS 50 MINUTES

INGREDIENTS:

- 1/3 cup water
- 4 1/2 tablespoons butter
- 4 1/2 eggs
- 3/8 cup sugar
- 3/4 teaspoon salt
- 1/3 teaspoon orange zest
- 1/8 teaspoon star anise
- 2 1/3 cups bread flour
- 1 1/2 teaspoons bread machine yeast

DIRECTIONS:

1. Whisk together the dry ingredients and set aside.
2. Add the liquid ingredients to the bread maker pan first, then gently pour the mixed dry ingredients on top of the liquid.
3. Set for Sweet bread cycle, medium crust color, and press Start.
4. Transfer to a cooling rack for 20 minutes before slicing to serve.

NUTRITIONAL INFO: CALORIES: 162, SODIUM: 172 MG, DIETARY Fiber: 0.6 g, Fat: 6.2 g, Carbs: 22.4 g, Protein: 4.4 g

Italian Bread

Soft Italian bread is absolutely delicious when served with your favorite meals. You can also create delicious sandwiches with your favorite cold cuts with this fresh-baked delicacy.

SERVINGS: 16 | PREP TIME: 5 MINUTES | COOK TIME: 3 HOURS 20 MINUTES

INGREDIENTS:

- 4 cups unbleached flour
- 1 tablespoon light brown sugar
- 1 1/3 cups warm water
- 1 1/2 teaspoons salt
- 1 1/2 teaspoons olive oil
- 1 package active dry yeast
- 1 egg
- 1 tablespoon water
- 2 tablespoons cornmeal

DIRECTIONS:

1. Add flour, brown sugar, warm water, salt, olive oil and yeast to the bread maker pan.
2. Select Dough cycle and press Start.
3. Punch down the dough and turn it out onto a lightly floured surface.
4. Form into two loaves and place them seam-side down on a cutting board.
5. Generously sprinkle with cornmeal and cover the loaves with a damp cloth.
6. Let rise until doubled in volume, about 40 minutes.
7. Beat egg and 1 tablespoon of water in a small mixing bowl.
8. Baste loaves with egg wash.
9. Cut down the center of loaves with a sharp knife.
10. Bake in 475°F preheated oven for 30 to 35 minutes, or until loaves sound hollow when tapped on the bottom.
11. Transfer to cooling rack for 15 minutes before serving.

NUTRITIONAL INFO: CALORIES: 128, SODIUM: 223 MG, DIETARY Fiber: 1 g, Fat: 1.1 g, Carbs: 25.3 g, Protein: 3.8 g

Russian Black Bread

A symbol of health and wealth, Russian black bread is best baked for times of celebration. It's also great as the base of Reuben sandwiches!

SERVINGS: 1 | PREP TIME: 5 MINUTES | COOK TIME: 3 HOURS

INGREDIENTS:

- 1 1/4 cups dark rye flour
- 2 1/2 cups unbleached flour
- 1 teaspoon instant coffee
- 2 tablespoons unsweetened cocoa powder
- 1 tablespoon whole caraway seeds
- 1/2 teaspoon dried minced onion
- 1/2 teaspoon fennel seeds
- 1 teaspoon sea salt
- 2 teaspoons active dry yeast
- 1 1/3 cups water, at room temperature

- 1 teaspoon sugar
- 1 1/2 tablespoons dark molasses
- 1 1/2 tablespoons apple cider vinegar
- 3 tablespoons vegetable oil

DIRECTIONS:

1. Mix dry ingredients together in a bowl, except for yeast.
2. Add wet ingredients to bread pan first; top with dry ingredients.
3. Make a well in the center of the dry ingredients and add the yeast.
4. Select Basic bread cycle, medium crust color, and press Start.
5. Let cool for 15 minutes before slicing.

NUTRITIONAL INFO: CALORIES: 169, SODIUM: 147 MG, DIETARY Fiber: 3.9 g, Fat: 3.9 g, Carbs: 29.8 g, Protein: 4.6 g

Mexican Sweet Bread

While the precise origin of this bread is unknown, it is a Mexican treat you'll quickly fall in love with. Serve with a cup of Mexican hot chocolate for a satisfying snack on a cold day.

SERVINGS: 12 | PREP TIME: 5 MINUTES | COOK TIME: 3 HOURS

INGREDIENTS:

- 1 cup whole milk
- 1/4 cup butter
- 1 egg
- 1/4 cup sugar
- 1 teaspoon salt
- 3 cups bread flour
- 1 1/2 teaspoons yeast

DIRECTIONS:

1. Add wet ingredients to bread maker pan.
2. Add dry ingredients, except yeast.
3. Make a well in the center of the dry ingredients and add the yeast.
4. Set to Sweet Bread cycle, light crust color, and press Start.
5. Remove to a cooling rack for 15 minutes before serving.

NUTRITIONAL INFO: CALORIES: 182, SODIUM: 235 MG, DIETARY Fiber: 1 g, Fat: 5.2 g, Carbs: 29.2 g, Protein: 4.6 g

Challah

A special Jewish bread, this loaf is soft and light and delicious on its own, or topped with just about any spread!

SERVINGS: 12 | PREP TIME: 15 MINUTES | COOK TIME: 1 HOUR 40 MINUTES

INGREDIENTS:

- 1/2 cup warm water
- 1 package active dry yeast
- 1 tablespoon sugar
- 3 tablespoons butter, softened
- 1/2 teaspoon kosher salt
- 2 to 2 1/2 cups kosher all-purpose flour
- 2 eggs
- 1 egg yolk
- 1 teaspoon water

DIRECTIONS:

1. Add sugar and salt to bread maker pan.
2. Add butter, eggs, then water.
3. Add flour and yeast.
4. Select Dough cycle and press Start.
5. Transfer dough to a large mixing bowl sprayed with non-stick cooking spray. Spray dough with non-stick cooking spray and cover. Let rise in a warm place until doubled in size; about 45 minutes.
6. Punch dough down. Remove dough to lightly floured surface; pat dough and shape into a 10-by-6-inch rectangle.
7. Divide into 3 equal strips with a pizza cutter. Braid strips and place into a 9-by-5-inch loaf pan sprayed with non-stick cooking spray. Cover and let rise in warm place for about 30 to 45 minutes.
8. Beat egg yolk with 1 teaspoon water and baste loaf.
9. Bake at 375°F for 25 to 30 minutes, or until golden.
10. Let cool on a rack for 5 minutes before removing from loaf pan and serve.

NUTRITIONAL INFO: CALORIES: 64, SODIUM: 129 MG, DIETARY Fiber: 0.3 g, Fat: 4 g, Carbs: 5.2 g, Protein: 1.9 g.

Russian Rye Bread

Slightly crumbly and tangy in taste, Russian Rye Bread is perfect for creamy dips or served toasted with sharp white cheddar cheese or labneh.

SERVINGS: 12 | PREP TIME: 5 MINUTES | COOK TIME: 3 HOURS

INGREDIENTS:

- 1 1/4 cups warm water
- 1 3/4 cups rye flour
- 1 3/4 cups whole wheat flour
- 2 tablespoons malt (or beer kit mixture)
- 1 tablespoon molasses
- 2 tablespoons white vinegar
- 1 teaspoon salt
- 1/2 tablespoon coriander seeds
- 1/2 tablespoon caraway seeds

- 2 teaspoons active dry yeast

DIRECTIONS:

1. Mix dry ingredients together in a bowl, except for yeast.
2. Add wet ingredients to bread pan first; top with dry ingredients.
3. Make a well in the center of the dry ingredients and add the yeast.
4. Press Basic bread cycle, choose medium crust color, and press Start.
5. Remove from bread pan and allow to cool on a wire rack before serving.

NUTRITIONAL INFO: CALORIES: 141, SODIUM: 196 MG, DIETARY Fiber: 5.1 g, Fat: 0.8 g, Carbs: 29.7 g, Protein: 5 g

Portuguese Corn Bread

Cook up a traditional taste of Portugal with this decadent, yet delicately sweet cornbread. Enjoy it with soups or buttered on its own.

SERVINGS: 8 | PREP TIME: 8 MINUTES | COOK TIME: 2 HOURS

INGREDIENTS:

- 1 cup yellow cornmeal
- 1 1/4 cups cold water, divided
- 1 1/2 teaspoons active dry yeast
- 1 1/2 cups bread flour
- 2 teaspoons sugar
- 3/4 teaspoon salt
- 1 tablespoon olive oil

DIRECTIONS:

1. Stir cornmeal into 3/4 cup of the cold water until lumps disappear.
2. Add cornmeal mixture and oil to bread maker pan.
3. Add remaining dry ingredients, except yeast, to pan.
4. Make a well in the center of the dry ingredients and add the yeast.
5. Choose Sweet bread cycle, light crust color and press Start.
6. Transfer to plate and serve warm.

NUTRITIONAL INFO: CALORIES: 108, SODIUM: 152 MG, DIETARY Fiber: 1.3 g, Fat: 1.7 g, Carbs: 20.6 g, Protein: 2.6 g

Amish Wheat Bread

Amish Wheat Bread is simple, moist, and easy to make in no time. Serve this hearty loaf with your favorite soups and salads.

SERVINGS: 12 | PREP TIME: 10 MINUTES | COOK TIME: 2 HOURS 50 MINUTES

INGREDIENTS:

- 1 1/8 cups warm water
- 1 package active dry yeast
- 2 3/4 cups wheat flour
- 1/2 teaspoon salt
- 1/3 cup sugar
- 1/4 cup canola oil
- 1 large egg

DIRECTIONS:

1. Add warm water, sugar and yeast to bread maker pan; let sit for 8 minutes or until it foams.
2. Add remaining ingredients to the pan.
3. Select Basic bread cycle, light crust color, and press Start.
4. Transfer to a cooling rack for 20 minutes before slicing.

NUTRITIONAL INFO: CALORIES: 173, SODIUM: 104 MG, DIETARY Fiber: 0.9 g, Fat: 5.3 g, Carbs: 27.7 g, Protein: 3.7 g

British Hot Cross Buns

Bake up a taste of Britain with these delicious buns, traditionally eaten at Easter. Be sure to serve them warm with a cup of English Breakfast tea and a spot of milk.

SERVINGS: 12 | PREP TIME: 20 MINUTES | COOK TIME: 2 HOURS 30 MINUTES

INGREDIENTS:

- 3/4 cup warm milk
- 3 tablespoons butter, unsalted
- 1/4 cup white sugar
- 1/2 teaspoon salt
- 1 egg
- 1 egg white
- 3 cups all-purpose flour
- 1 tablespoon active dry yeast
- 3/4 cup dried raisins

- 1 teaspoon ground cinnamon
- For Brushing:
- 1 egg yolk
- 2 tablespoons water
- For the Crosses:
- 2 tablespoons flour
- Cold water
- 1/2 tablespoon sugar

DIRECTIONS:

1. Put milk, butter, 1/4 cup sugar, salt, egg, egg white, flour, and yeast in bread maker and start the Dough cycle.
2. Add raisins and cinnamon 5 minutes before kneading cycle ends.
3. Allow to rest in machine until doubled, about 30 minutes.
4. Punch down on a floured surface, cover, and let rest 10 minutes.
5. Shape into 12 balls and place in a greased 9-by-12-inch pan.
6. Cover and let rise in a warm place until doubled, about 35-40 minutes.
7. Mix egg yolk and 2 tablespoons water and baste each bun.
8. Mix the cross ingredients to form pastry.
9. Roll out pastry and cut into thin strips. Place across the buns to form crosses.
10. Bake at 375°F for 20 minutes.
11. Remove from pan immediately and cool on a rack. Serve warm.

NUTRITIONAL INFO: CALORIES: 200, SODIUM: 135 MG, DIETARY Fiber: 1.5 g, Fat: 4 g, Carbs: 36.5 g, Protein: 5.2 g

Hawaiian Bread

Sweet Hawaiian bread is out of this world! This bread makes delicious sandwiches and even French toast.

SERVINGS: 12 | PREP TIME: 5 MINUTES | COOK TIME: 3 HOURS

INGREDIENTS:

- 3/4 cup pineapple juice
- 1 egg
- 2 tablespoons olive oil
- 2 tablespoons whole milk
- 2 1/2 tablespoons sugar
- 3/4 teaspoon salt
- 3 cups bread flour
- 1 1/2 teaspoons active dry yeast

DIRECTIONS:

1. Add the wet ingredients to bread maker pan, then add sugar, salt and flour.
2. Make a well in the center of the dry ingredients and add the yeast
3. Press Basic bread cycle, choose medium crust color, and press Start.
4. Remove from bread pan and allow to cool before serving.

NUTRITIONAL INFO: CALORIES: 160, SODIUM: 155 MG, DIETARY Fiber: 1 g, Fat: 3.1 g, Carbs: 28.7 g, Protein: 4 g

Greek Easter Bread

Tsoureki is a traditional bread served at Easter in Greece. You'll love this quick and easy way to bake this traditional holiday bread.

SERVINGS: 12 | PREP TIME: 20 MINUTES | COOK TIME: 3 HOURS

INGREDIENTS:

- 2/3 cup fresh butter
- 1 cup milk
- 1 cup sugar
- 1 teaspoon mastic
- 1/2 teaspoon salt
- 1 package active dry yeast
- 3 eggs
- 5 cups strong yellow flour
- 1 egg, for brushing blended with 1 teaspoon water

DIRECTIONS:

1. Heat milk and butter until melted in a saucepan; do not boil. Add to bread maker pan.
2. Add sugar and mastic to a food processor and blend; add to bread maker pan.
3. Add remaining ingredients.
4. Set Dough cycle and press Start; leave dough to rise one hour after cycle.
5. Shape into 2 loaves, cover, and leave to rise for 50 more minutes.
6. Baste with egg wash.
7. Bake at 320°F for 30 to 40 minutes or until golden brown.
8. Transfer to cooling rack for 15 minutes before serving.

NUTRITIONAL INFO: CALORIES: 554, SODIUM: 182 MG, DIETARY Fiber: 2.8 g, Fat: 12.9 g, Carbs: 97.6 g, Protein: 13.4 g

Fiji Sweet Potato Bread

Sweet potato bread is hearty and dense. Best served with savory meats, you'll love this satisfying and nourishing taste of Fiji.

SERVINGS: 12 | PREP TIME: 5 MINUTES | COOK TIME: 3 HOURS

INGREDIENTS:

- 1 1/4 cups sweet potato, mashed
- 10 tablespoons canned coconut milk
- 1 teaspoon ginger, fresh grated
- 1 tablespoon lemon zest
- 2 tablespoons honey
- 2 tablespoons olive oil
- 3 cups bread flour
- 1 teaspoon salt
- 2 1/4 teaspoons rapid rise yeast

DIRECTIONS:

1. Add the wet ingredients to bread maker pan.
2. Mix dry ingredients, except for yeast, in a bowl. Add to pan.
3. Make a well in the center of the dry ingredients and add the yeast.
4. Press Basic bread cycle, choose medium crust color, and press Start.
5. Remove from bread pan and allow to cool before serving.

NUTRITIONAL INFO: CALORIES: 193, SODIUM: 204 MG, DIETARY Fiber: 2 g, Fat: 5.5 g, Carbs: 32.2 g, Protein: 4.2 g

Za'atar Bread

Whip up a taste of the Middle East with this delicious and perfectly seasoned bread. Serve with hummus and your favorite kebabs.

SERVINGS: 12 - 14 | PREP TIME: 5 MINUTES | COOK TIME: 3 HOURS

INGREDIENTS:

- 1/3 cup za'atar seasoning
- 2 tablespoons onion powder
- 1 cup warm water
- 2 tablespoons agave nectar
- 1/4 cup applesauce
- 3 cups bread flour
- 1 teaspoon salt
- 2 1/4 teaspoons rapid rise yeast

DIRECTIONS:

1. Mix dry ingredients together in a bowl, except for yeast.
2. Add wet ingredients to bread pan first; top with dry ingredients.
3. Make a well in the center of the dry ingredients and add the yeast.
4. Press Basic bread cycle, choose medium crust color, and press Start.
5. Remove from bread pan and allow to cool before serving.

NUTRITIONAL INFO: CALORIES: 125, SODIUM: 196 MG, DIETARY Fiber: 2 g, Fat: 1.2 g, Carbs: 24.6 g, Protein: 4.1 g

CPSIA information can be obtained
at www.ICGtesting.com
Printed in the USA
BVHW091049180321
602887BV00010B/1195